REASONABLE FAITH:

The Scientific Case for Christianity

by

D0109217

Dr. Jay L. Wile, Ph.D.

This work is dedicated to my loving wife, Kathleen Wile

"Thank God for you, the wind beneath my wings"

William,
I really
hope you like
it!
Dr. Jay L. Wile
1 Peter 3:15

Reasonable Faith

Manufactured in the United States of America
Second Printing 1998

Published By
Apologia Educational Ministries
Anderson, IN

Printed by
BookCrafters USA, Inc.
Chelsea, MI

TABLE OF CONTENTS

Reasonable Faith:
The Scientific Case for Christianity

Foreword
Dr. Charles R. Purdy, M. D.

As we come to the close of this millennium, we find American society in a very unique situation. There are no prevailing philosophies, and most of the established paradigms have become stale. We have enjoyed decades of relative prosperity and peace. The Cold War is over. There is very little to stir our emotion or energy. The church finds itself confronting a society that holds to few absolutes. The scientific foundation for life science education in the universities has been based on Darwinian evolution for several decades now. The human being is understood now in mechanistic terms. Our scientists have given us a wealth of information about the elemental biochemical makeup of the human body.

Medicine has provided cures for most of the diseases that plagued humanity in centuries gone by. Small Pox is but a distant memory. Tuberculosis asylums have been out of business for over forty years. Very few people die from pneumonia. We have *designer drugs* that can very specifically address almost any ailment.

We see so much advancement at a time when the social fabric of our society is being tested as never before. It seems that with this explosion of scientific knowledge, we have somehow lost touch with the spiritual side of mankind. That element of life that held such a central place in societies of past ages seems to be completely absent. Could it be that mankind is crying out for something more? Is it possible that the mechanistic approach to explaining the phenomenon of mankind is not enough?

Many of us in the scientific community have asked these questions. As a physician, I follow a scientific approach to understanding and treating disease, yet I frequently find that something is lacking when man's spiritual needs are neglected. Several years ago as the Christmas season was approaching, a beautiful middle-aged woman came to my office complaining of a nagging cough. She had suffered from this cough for several weeks. As part of her evaluation, I ordered a chest X-ray. Later that same day I was called by the radiologist. His voice had a low, ominous tone. He explained that there was a suspicious mass seen in the left mid lung field. The likely diagnosis was cancer. My heart sank. How could this be? The patient was only fifty years old, and she was not a smoker. The following morning I had the difficult task of explaining to this woman that she had lung cancer. As I gave her this information, a solemn quiet fell over the exam room. She confessed that this news would make the holiday season very difficult to get through. She went on to explain that her mother had been diagnosed with lung cancer just before Christmas when she was the same age. She had survived only a few months.

Over the next several weeks, I saw the patient frequently in the office. It had been readily determined that the tumor was inoperable. She was enrolled in an aggressive program of radiation therapy. Though she was very devoted to following the directives of her physicians, nothing seemed to help. The cancer progressed in an unrelenting fashion.

I don't remember the exact day, but there was a point when we realized the limitations of what we were attempting. I turned to her and asked her if I could pray for her. It became obvious to me that the spiritual side of this woman was crying out for hope. I prayed that God would miraculously heal her. I pleaded with God to intervene in the physiological battle that was being lost in her body. From this experience, I found a greater assurance of God's presence and abiding love for each one of us. My patient found comfort and hope in my prayer to an omnipotent God. From this experience, she also found that it was okay to loosen her trust in the powers of modern medicine. As her physician, I had given her permission to look beyond what I could offer, to look beyond what science could offer.

The weeks that followed were not without their moments of fear and despair, yet there was a calmness and peace in this woman that I had not seen before. God chose not to heal this woman. The radiation therapy help to slow the progression, yet the cancer won in the end. I stood at her bedside as she was dying. After she had lapsed into a coma, I realized the emptiness of the purely scientific explanation to our purpose and existence. I saw clearly that we as members of the scientific community had an obligation to acknowledge that truth about the world that we live in.

In late 1996, I had the privilege of reviewing a preliminary manuscript of *Reasonable Faith*. I was encouraged by what I found. This work provided a systematic and scholarly approach to discussing the Christian faith. It offered a logical link between modern science and faith in a loving God.

As a pre-med student at the University of Illinois, I was first exposed to the evolution-based approach to life sciences. As a young Christian, I was intimidated by the animosity that I found toward religion in general, and Christianity in particular. I was amazed at the defensiveness of the educators as they taught that evolution was the only possible explanation of man's origins. Perhaps the Scopes trial early in the century made them feel that if any ground was given to the Creationist argument, they would be back to fighting off the unreasonable religious masses. The educators at the University seemed to like an environment of very little competition. This is human nature; we dislike being pushed to work harder than we have to.

Since my goal was to become a family doctor, I knew I had to persevere in that intolerant environment, so I learned the evolution-based approach to life science. This experience continued throughout my medical training. There was always a great deal of discomfort in dealing with what are considered religious issues. There was little room given to addressing the spiritual needs of patients. Yet ironically, in day to day office practice, I see that the spiritual side of mankind is always interacting with the physical, emotional, and mental sides. Sometimes the primary problem a patient struggles with is spiritual in nature. I wish Dr. Wile's *Reasonable Faith* had been available to me during my years of formal training.

This book provides a rich resource of sound apologetic material. It begins with a scientific argument in support of creation and a creator. It then moves on to provide a scholarly and logical argument in support of the Bible. Chapters 7 and 8 lay a very strong foundation for believing that Jesus Christ was a true historical figure and the He indeed was the Son of God. It helps to show that Jesus was not just a myth; He was who He said He was. All arguments are backed up with references at the end of each chapter.

Reasonable Faith provides a very concise, readable scientific explanation of the Christian faith. Though no one would say that his faith is based totally on reason, I think that it is reasonable to believe that if Christianity is true, there should be some reason and common sense to what it proclaims. Students in a university setting are eager to open their minds and learn the truth. They don't want to be preached to, nor fed religious propaganda. I believe that many would be willing to ponder the arguments that this text presents. I would argue that this material would be an appropriate addition to any university's life science curriculum. Even if one doesn't agree with the conclusions made, I think that he would have to agree that the author makes a very sound case in support of the Christian faith.

For someone searching for truth and answers about our world, I would heartily recommend *Reasonable Faith*. While the author carefully references and footnotes all supporting background literature, he also achieves a flowing, readable style that carries the reader from chapter to chapter. The obvious place of a designer and creator emerges as the argument unfolds. Like walking on a spring morning to see the beauty of nature; the sounds, the smells, and the sights all around, this book opens one's mind to what many have known all along. That we are not alone. That we are not destined to a life of no meaning. That there is a true focus of love in the universe.

I would encourage you to sit down this evening with a cup of coffee and begin the journey through this important work. If you are not a Christian, I would simply ask you to open your mind to the material submitted. Try to set aside any preset bias against the faith and consider each of the arguments. You have nothing to lose. If you are a believer, I would encourage you to let this material strengthen and solidify your faith. If there is truly a God up there, and if He loved us enough to sacrifice His only Son, He will provide a way for you to see Him. You will see him not just through the eyes of faith, but also through the eyes of reason and understanding. Belief, planted firmly in the soil of reason, will withstand the winds of time.

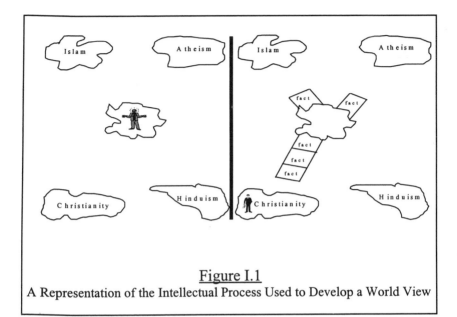

<u>Figure I.1</u>
A Representation of the Intellectual Process Used to Develop a World View

When a person begins trying to determine what to believe, he is like a man on an island. The island is surrounded by water: the sea of ideas. He has in his possession several facts, and he needs to decide what to believe based on those facts. The facts usually come from life experiences, observations of others, or formal education. As he looks out, he can see several other islands. One island might represent the Islamic religion; another might represent atheism; another might represent Christianity; and so on. In order to adopt one of these world views, he must move to the appropriate island. At first, it looks like he must make a giant leap (a leap of faith) to get from his island to any of the others.

However, instead of making a giant leap of faith across the sea of ideas, the person begins using his facts to build bridges to each of the islands. For example, perhaps he has read about all of the Islamic fundamentalists that are willing to die for what they believe. This might be a fact which supports the validity of the Islamic religion. Perhaps the person knows that atheism is very popular among scientists; he may use that as a fact supporting atheism. The more facts that seem to support a given idea, the closer the bridge gets to the island that represents that idea. In the end, the person will end up heading towards the island which has the longest bridge running to it. He still must leap from the end of the bridge onto the island, but the leap of faith will be short when the bridge of facts leading to the idea is long.

In fact, this is how scientists decide which scientific theories to believe. The more experimental evidence that "stacks up" in favor of a given theory, the easier it is to believe. For example, it is impossible (baring some mind-boggling technological miracle) for science to ever prove that atoms, the fundamental building blocks of nature, are really made up of protons, neutrons, and electrons. However, atomic theory has so many facts stacked up in its favor, that it is very hard to believe otherwise. In my opinion, Christianity is very similar to atomic theory. Despite the fact that the validity of the Christian faith can never be proven, when one begins stacking up the facts, it is hard not to believe in Christianity.

In the following pages, I attempt to present the facts that stack up in favor of Christianity. First, I will argue that science provides incredibly convincing evidence that God exists. Like in most things, science does not *prove* God's existence; it merely makes it very difficult to believe otherwise. After you've seen the evidence for the existence of God, I will present evidence that the God which science points to is really the Christian God. The evidence I present will be based on scientific fact and logical reasoning. If, in the end, the evidence is not convincing, I wholeheartedly believe that the fault lies with the writer, not with the scientific case for Christianity.

Chapter 1
The Argument From Design

A scientist's main job is to collect a number of facts and try to formulate theories based on those facts. The theories that he formulates must be useful in explaining the nature of the world around us, and they must be consistent with all of the facts at hand. For example, suppose a scientist were walking across a desert. The desert is rather featureless-a sand dune here, a spiny cactus there. Suddenly, in the middle of the desert, our scientist stumbles across a watch. Being a curious person, he picks it up and begins to examine it.

As our scientist looks at the watch, he could develop theories as to how the watch came to be in the desert. One theory would be that the watch simply formed itself out of the raw materials in the desert. It is possible that, by some happy coincidence, all of the chemical elements that make up the watch simply collided and formed all of the various components which make the watch work. This theory might be called the "chance theory."

Another theory might be that the watch was designed and made by another person and was then simply lost in the desert. We could call this the "design theory." Which theory is more scientifically sound? In order to answer this question, the scientist begins looking at the facts. Whichever theory is supported by the most facts is probably the more scientifically sound theory.

In starting his collection of facts, the first thing our scientist does is examine the chemical makeup of both the watch and the desert. He sees that all of the chemical elements in the watch are, in fact, in the desert as well. This seems to be a fact in favor of the chance theory.

Of course, this fact alone is not enough for our thorough scientist, so he begins more data collection. He examines the watch and sees that the watch contains some intricate electronic circuitry, light emitting diodes (LEDs), a small crystal of quartz, and a battery. The battery is connected to the crystal which vibrates back and forth. He begins to count the vibrations of the crystal and realizes that after a certain number of them, the electronic circuitry sends a pulse to the LEDs which makes the seconds display increase by one. After 60 such pulses, the seconds display returns to zero and the minutes display increases by one. After 60 minutes, the hours display increases by one while both the seconds and the minutes displays are set back to zero. This process continues for 24 hours until everything is set back to zero and the process begins again.

As the scientist begins to review all of the facts that he has collected, the chance theory becomes less and less likely an explanation of the watch's existence. After all, the regularity and precision with which all of the components of the watch work together is quite amazing. If any one part of the watch were to be absent or not working, the entire watch would cease operating properly.

Being a well-trained scientist, he also sees that simply having all of the necessary parts in working order is still not enough to ensure that the watch will run properly. Each component must be finely tuned to the others. For example, if the battery in the watch were of too high a voltage, the watch would run fast. If, instead, the voltage were too low, the watch would run slow. Each resistor and capacitor in the electronic circuitry is tuned to the transistor that they protect. If the resistors and capacitors were much bigger or smaller, the transistors in the circuitry would cease to function. Once all of these facts are reviewed, it is clear that the watch is far too well-designed to have appeared by chance. Thus, the facts seem to support the theory that the watch had a designer and builder.

The world in which we live is similar in nature to a watch. There are, literally, millions of processes working together to make life possible on earth. If any one of these processes were to stop, life on earth would abruptly come to an end. The processes are all finely-tuned to one another to provide the perfect situation for life as we know it. In fact, all of the design elements that one sees in a modern-day watch are exceedingly simple compared to those processes which run our planet and the life therein. Thus, if it is self-evident that a simple watch must have a designer and builder, it is even more self-evident that life itself must also have a designer and builder. That's what we call "God."

This argument is not new. William Paley[1], an eighteenth century British naturalist and theologian, used this argument in his book, *Natural Theology on Evidence and Attributes of Deity*. Of course, the watch that Paley referred to was a mechanical one, not the electronic one discussed above, but the final conclusion remains the same. Even with the limited scientific knowledge accumulated in the eighteenth century, it was clear that the earth was a product of design, not chance.

Of course, our knowledge of the world around us has increased significantly since the eighteenth century. Instead of weakening Paley's argument, however, modern science has strengthened it even further. It is truly amazing how much evidence has accumulated over the years in favor of the design theory. The next four chapters attempt to outline just a few of the incredible scientific facts that point very strongly to the theory that our world was designed. However, before investigating these facts, we must first examine three objections which scientists and philosophers have raised against Paley's argument.

The "Natural Selection" Argument

In 1859, Charles Darwin published one of the most influential works in the history of science, *The Origin of Species*. In this book, Darwin attempted to explain the origin of the various biological species on earth by a process which he called "natural selection." According to Darwin, the apparent design that we see in biological systems today is not the result of a designer, instead, it is the result of nature continually trying out new systems. As these systems are tested, Nature throws away the ones that don't work and keeps the ones that do.

Darwin believed that through the process of reproduction, new attributes were always surfacing amongst the various life forms on the earth. If a new attribute caused a life form to be weaker, slower, less intelligent, or less likely to reproduce, the life form would die off quickly, and the new attribute would be lost. Instead, if the new attribute made the life form more fit to survive, then it would be more likely to pass on that new attribute to all future generations. As time went on, more and more new attributes would be introduced.

As these new attributes combined, species would become more and more different and complex. Thus, when we look at the world around us today, we are actually looking at the results of this natural selection working over millions and millions of years.

It's important to realize that Darwin was not an anti-religion crusader. He did not propose his theory as part of a preconceived plan to undermine the church. Instead, he was a strong Christian before he began his scientific investigations. In *The Life and Letters of Charles Darwin*, he is quoted as writing, "...I did not then in the least doubt the strict and literal truth of every word in the Bible."[2] As he started his investigations, however, his scientific theory began to erode his faith in the literal interpretation of scripture. He struggled with himself as to whether or not to publish his theory because he knew the effect it would have on the church. In the end, however, he felt that the scientific importance of his theory could not be ignored, and he decided to publish his work.

The struggle that existed in Darwin's mind can be best illustrated by his reaction to a letter written to him by his wife. In that letter, she asked him not to publish his book because it would hurt the church. After Darwin's death, the letter was discovered among his personal effects. It was worn from excessive handling[3] and, scribbled at the bottom, he had written, "When I am dead, know that many times I have kissed and cried over this."[4] This comment indicates that Darwin was certainly not the anti-religion crusader that many have tried to make him. Instead, he was a scientist who was reluctant to promote his work, because of the disastrous effect in would have on the church.[5]

Of course, others were not as reluctant as Darwin to use scientific theories against the church. Many in the scientific community wanted to get God completely out of science, and they used Darwin's theory as a means to that end. In God's place, they put the concept of random chance. Yes, they conceded, the world around us does look like it was designed. But this apparent design is really just the result of millions upon millions of years of random chance acted upon by natural selection.

At first, they say, there was no life on earth. However, many of the simple chemicals that existed at that time were randomly colliding with each other. Because of natural energy sources such as

4

thermal springs, volcanoes, lightning, and ultra-violet light, these collisions were often quite violent. Through billions of years of blind chance, eventually some of these simple chemicals collided in just the right way to produce the chemicals that eventually led to life.

The life form that resulted from this blind arrangements of molecules was probably some kind of very, very simple single-celled creature. As this creature began to produce offspring, mistakes were sometimes made in the reproductive process. These mistakes, called mutations, caused some of the offspring to have significantly different features than those of their parent. Most of the time, these new features harmed the overall survivability of the offspring, so they died out. However, every once in a while, a "beneficial" mutation occurred which caused the offspring to be more fit to survive. This organism would then survive and pass its new feature on to all of its offspring. As these new features began piling up, the offspring looked very, very different from the ancestor. In this way, single-celled life forms became multi-celled life forms. Multi-celled life forms became more and more complex until they became simple aquatic vertebrates like fish. These fish later evolved into amphibians, and so on. This process is assumed to be responsible for all of the diversity and complexity in life that we see on earth today.

Using this argument, evolutionary scientists would like us to believe that the apparent design that we see in our world is really just the product of random chance, guided by natural selection. Much can be said, however, to refute this argument. First, there is a growing skepticism, even within the scientific community, that such evolution ever really occurred. A detailed discussion of such a topic is beyond the scope of this book. However, several other authors have written in detail concerning this subject,[6-8] and they demonstrate that there is very little empirical evidence supporting the natural selection argument. In addition, many of the living creatures that we will discuss in chapter 5 simply cannot be explained by reference to natural selection.

The most obvious objection that can be leveled against the theory of apparent design through natural selection, however, is the fact that natural selection can only occur in *living* systems. The concepts of survivability and passing on traits to offspring are applicable only to systems that are already alive. Thus, in order to have natural selection, we must first have life. Contrary to what scientists used to think, we now know that there is *no such thing as a simple life form*. Even the "simple" one-celled creatures that we see today are exceedingly complex. Since natural selection can only operate on living systems, it cannot explain the all-important leap from non-living chemicals to living systems.[9] Thus, natural selection notwithstanding, our earlier analogy to the watch still holds.

As we will see in the next chapter, in order to form life from non-life, several complex chemical systems must come together and work in concert. Each system must be finely-tuned to the others. If one system is absent or not working, then life will not exist. Natural selection simply cannot operate until life is created. Thus, natural selection cannot explain the complex arrangements we see in the simplest life forms here on earth nor can it explain why earth is so perfectly suited to support this life.

The "No Surprise" Argument

Another objection often brought up against the argument from design is the "no surprise" argument. Proponents of this position say that we should not be surprised at the incredible complexity of the world around us. After all, the mere fact that we can observe our surroundings means that life did, in fact evolve. No matter how impossible the evolution of such a complex system may be, it nevertheless happened, or we wouldn't be around to talk about it. Since it is obvious that life did, indeed, evolve, we should concentrate on learning how it evolved instead of wasting our time discussing whether or not it evolved.

The deficiency of this argument is quite clear. It starts out with an assumption that evolution is the only way that life could be produced on earth. It ignores any other possibilities, such as supernatural involvement. In the end, the proper way to construct this argument is to say that since we know life exists today, it either (a) was the result of a wildly impossible coincidence or (b) was the result of supernatural creation. Both of these conclusions may be unpalatable at first, because a person might see both of them as highly unlikely. But now that the argument has been correctly phrased, it becomes clear what the rational person must do. He must investigate both possibilities and see which one is the more scientifically sound conclusion.

For example, suppose a man is sentenced to death and put before a firing squad. He looks at the line of 12 people standing in front of him, and he sees that they all have their rifles pointing straight at him. The commander gives the order to fire, and the man hears the rifles fire. He then is surprised to find himself still alive! He checks his body for bullet holes and he is amazed to find none! He looks at the situation and wonders how he could still be alive. Is it possible that everyone in the firing squad simply missed? The proponents of the "no surprise" objection would say "yes." The fact that he can still see, hear, and feel indicates that he is alive and therefore it should come as no surprise that the bullets didn't hit him. Thus, even though it is wildly improbable, the 12 marksmen who were aiming at point blank range must have all missed!

This conclusion, of course, would be absurd. There are other possible explanations for the fact that the man is still alive. Contrary to the proponents of the "no surprise" argument, these possibilities must be investigated. Perhaps the commander was sympathetic towards the man and ordered his firing squad to aim away from him at the very last second. Perhaps one of the man's friends slipped into the marksmen's barracks at night and replaced their bullets with blanks. Perhaps this was all just an intricate practical joke. In any event, the conclusion that all of the marksmen had missed is certainly not the most rational conclusion to reach. Other possibilities are more likely and must be considered. The same holds true for the question of how life originated. There are many possibilities for explaining how life occurred, and a truly rational person must consider all of them to reach the correct answer.

The bad-design argument

Stephen Jay Gould, arguably the world's leading evolutionist, has offered another objection to Paley's argument from design. In his book, *The Panda's Thumb*, Gould says that there are things in nature that are very poorly designed[10]. If an intelligent, powerful being had really designed the world we live in, then surely these badly designed systems wouldn't exist. In essence, Gould is saying that because some of nature's work looks a bit "slip-shod," then random chance *must* be the explanation, because an intelligent, all-powerful designer would never let such slip-shod work into his marvelous creation.

First, we must rebut his argument, which is very simple. In fact, each example of bad design that he presents is actually only bad in his eyes. For example, Gould highlights a bad design feature which he thinks is apparent in the case of the giant panda. These interesting mammals eat primarily bamboo. In order to exist on such a diet, the pandas must have a means of grasping the bamboo shoot and stripping it of its leaves. Since pandas belong to the order Carnivora, however, they do not have opposable thumbs. Instead, a bone in the panda's wrist (the radial sesamoid) is extended and serves as a partial "thumb" which gives the panda the ability to grasp and manipulate bamboo shoots. Gould thinks that this design is so awkward it could only have developed by chance. Any decent engineer would do a much better job at designing a thumb for the panda. Thus, Gould thinks that the panda's thumb is such a strong argument against the existence of a Creator, he features it as the title of his book.

However, many other experts consider the panda's thumb to be perfectly designed for its purpose. According to Dr. Duane T. Gish, the panda "...uses it extremely effectively to strip the leaves off of bamboo."[11] The panda doesn't need a real thumb; it only needs a device which it can use to grasp its food and prepare it to be eaten. The "thumb" which it has is perfectly designed for this purpose. If a panda needed to tie shoelaces or drive a nail with a hammer, then the thumb which it has would certainly be unsuitable. The panda, however, does need to do these things. It merely needs to grab bamboo shoots and strip them of their leaves. The panda's thumb does just that and does it very effectively. Thus, Gould's objection cannot stand up to the light of fact.

Before we leave this objection, it is important to note that in raising this point, Gould has unwittingly supported the case for the existence of a Creator. He admits that random chance guided by natural selection should not develop intricate, exquisite life forms. Instead, any life form made as the result of random chance should, indeed, look rather slip-shod. The very fact that Gould could only find a few examples of such poor design and the fact that those examples seem to only be valid in his eyes strongly support the idea that random chance cannot be used to explain the origin of life as we know it.

One final note

Before we leave this chapter, I want to address one philosophical objection that can be raised against the argument from design. Some atheists claim that the argument from design is really simply an argument from ignorance. They say that proponents of the argument look at the intricately-designed world around them and say that they have no idea where such elegant design could come from, therefore it must come from God. This, the atheists say, is no different than the cave-man who, upon looking at the sun, could find no explanation for it and therefore concluded that the sun must be a god.

In principle, I agree with this objection. The argument from design is, in fact, an admission that we can only explain the intricate, elegant world around us by putting faith in the existence of a designer, whom we have never seen. I ask you for a moment, however, to consider the alternative. When asked how they might explain the incredible design and complexity of the world around them, atheists will say that it is possible for order (or design) to spring up spontaneously, given enough time. The design that we see around us is the result of this spontaneous generation of order working in tandem with natural selection. So, in order to explain the intricate, elegant world around them, atheists put their faith in the spontaneous generation of order, which they have never seen. Both theists and atheists are putting their faith in something: theists put their faith in God, atheists put their faith in the hope that order can spontaneously appear from chaos.

It is clear, however, that faith in a designer is more scientifically sound than the alternative. After all, we see the effects of a designer's work all around us. We see buildings, ships, televisions, watches, and many more intricately-designed systems. We know that each of these systems has a designer; thus, it is not a very big step of faith to believe that the intricately designed world we live in must also have a designer. We have never experienced the spontaneous generation of order, however. In fact, many scientists believe that the second law of thermodynamics forbids such a thing from ever occurring![12]   Clearly, then, the idea that order can spontaneously appear from chaos has no facts supporting it, and perhaps has one fact contradicting it. Instead, the idea that the earth has a designer is supported by our experiences in everyday life. It is quite clear which of the two "faiths" is the most scientifically sound.

Now that we have discussed the objections against the argument from design, it is time to examine the scientific evidence for this argument. In the next three chapters, I will outline a tiny fraction of the countless design features that exist in nature.   In chapter five, I will then present some of the most amazing life forms that exist on this planet. They all have design features that simply cannot be explained in the framework of the theory of evolution. After chapter five, the scientific case for the existence of God will be complete. From there, I will present the evidence that supports the fact that this God is the God of the Bible.

ENDNOTES

1. William Paley, *Natural Theology on Evidence and Attributes of Deity*, 18th ed., Lackinton, Allen and Co:Edinburgh, UK 1818.

2. Michael Denton, *Evolution: A Theory in Crisis*, Adler and Adler:Bethesda, MD 1986, p.25.

3. Richard Milner, *The Encyclopedia of Evolution*, Facts on File: New York, NY 1990, p. 116.

4. Denton, p. 55.

5. Milner, pp.108-118.

6. Denton, *op. cit.*

7. Duane T. Gish, *Evolution: The Challenge of the Fossil Record*, Master Books:El Cajon, CA 1986.

8. Henry M. Morris and Gary E. Parker, *What is Creation Science?*, Mater Books:El Cajon, CA 1987.

9. Charles B. Thaxton, *et al.*, *The Mystery of Life's Origin: Reassessing Current Theories*, Philosophical Library:New York, NY 1984.

10. Stephen J. Gould, *The Panda's Thumb*, Norton:New York, NY 1980.

11. Duane T. Gish, *Creation Scientists Answer Their Critics*, Master Books:El Cajon, CA 1993.

12. Robert Gange, *Origins and Destiny*, Word:Dallas, TX 1986, pp. 33-40.

Chapter 2
Let's Start Small

In order to get a deep appreciation for the intricate design that exists in even the "simplest" life form on earth, we must first know a little bit about the fundamental building blocks of the universe: atoms. Atoms are incredibly small; so small that they cannot be seen with the human eye, no matter how powerful a microscope is used. In fact, there are roughly 100,000,000,000,000,000,000 atoms contained in the head of a pin. Despite the fact that atoms are so small, they make up all of the things that we see in the world around us. From a lump of iron to a Corvette sports car, all things are composed of atoms.

Marvelously enough, these tiny atoms are composed of even smaller things called protons, neutrons, and electrons. A very simplistic picture of the atom is shown in the figure below.

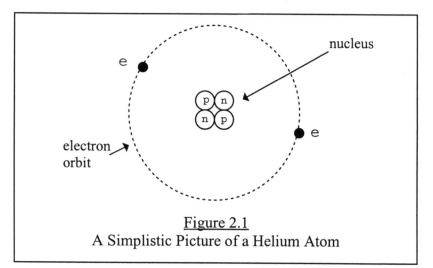

Figure 2.1
A Simplistic Picture of a Helium Atom

In this figure, neutrons (n) and protons (p) exist in the center of the atom, which is called the nucleus. Outside the nucleus, electrons (e) whirl around in circular orbits.[1] It is very interesting to point out that this picture *cannot* be drawn to scale. The electrons are actually much, much farther away from the nucleus than what is drawn in the figure. If the nucleus of an atom really were the size that is shown in the figure, then the electrons would be roughly 1.5 miles away from it.

Thus, the first thing we see about atoms is that they are composed mostly of empty space. This is true of all matter. Although you may not believe it, the book that you are currently reading is about 99.999999999999997% empty space.[2] The reason that this book doesn't feel like empty space is a bit too complex to explain here.

Each type of atom in the universe has a specific number of protons, neutrons, and electrons. For example, the atom pictured in the figure is a helium atom. When you fill a balloon with helium so that it will float, you are putting almost 100,000,000,000,000,000,000,000 of these atoms into it. If there were a different number of neutrons, protons, or electrons, it would be a different atom. Life as we know it is based on carbon atoms. Carbon atoms contain six protons, six electrons, and six neutrons[3]. So, in order to build up the chemicals that define life, we must first properly arrange protons, neutrons, and electrons into various atoms.

It turns out that the proton is approximately 1,000 times heavier than the electron, whereas the neutron is only about 0.1% heavier than the proton. These mass differences are critically important. For example, if the neutron were just another 0.1% heavier than the proton, then protons would spontaneously turn into neutrons. This would deplete the universe of protons. Since all atoms need at least one proton in them, there would be *absolutely no atoms in the entire universe* if the mass of the neutron were even a little greater than it actually is[4]! Isn't it amazing that the mass difference between the neutron and proton just happens to be enough to ensure the existence of atoms?

In addition, the mass difference between the proton and the electron is also critically important. In order to form complex chemicals, atoms bond together to form molecules. Atoms form these bonds by sharing each other's electrons. For example, the natural gas that most people burn in their stove is composed of one carbon atom sharing electrons with 4 hydrogen atoms. This gas molecule, CH_4, gets its ability to burn from the arrangement and bonding of the carbon and hydrogen atoms. If another atom were added to the molecule or if an atom were taken away, the resulting molecule would have completely different chemical properties.

If electrons were much heavier than they are presently, then they would orbit the nucleus significantly closer than they do now. If that were the case, it would inhibit the ability of atoms to bond with each other[5], making it impossible for complex, life-giving molecules to form. If electrons were significantly lighter, then they would orbit much farther away from the nucleus, and it would be very easy to pull them away from the atom. If this were the case, then atoms would be less inclined to share electrons and more inclined to take them from each other[6]. This would make it impossible for even the simplest life-giving molecule to form!

There are even more intricate design features in the atom. It also turns out that protons are electrically charged. In fact, they are positively charged. Electrons, on the other hand, are negatively charged, whereas neutrons have no electrical charge whatsoever. Once again, these charges must be very well-balanced in order to ensure the existence of atoms. Despite the fact that the proton is 1,000 times heavier than the electron, it has exactly as much positive charge as the electron has negative charge. This allows the electrical charge of the proton to offset the electrical charge of the electron. Since all atoms have equal numbers of electrons and protons, they are electrically neutral. If this were not the case, there would be disastrous consequences. For example, calculations indicate that if the proton and electron charges were different by as little as 0.00000001%, the resulting electrical imbalance in our bodies would cause us to instantaneously explode![7]

The most important thing to realize is that these atoms are the *simplest* building blocks of life. Even these very simple building blocks, however, have delicately balanced parts which all work together to give the atom its properties. If one of these parts were even slightly altered, the delicate balance would be destroyed and the chemistry necessary for life would be forever lost. Of course, this is only the beginning. As atoms start bonding together to make life-giving chemicals, things just start getting more complex, and earth's design features become even more apparent.

All life-giving molecules involve carbon atoms bonding to other types of atoms. In general, such molecules are referred to as "organic" molecules. Thus, in order to form the organic molecules necessary for life, there must be a significant amount of carbon available in the universe. In addition, the chemical reactions which give most life forms the energy necessary for survival are simple combustion reactions. In order to have combustion reactions, there needs to be a plentiful supply of oxygen.

In Figure 2.2, the relative abundance of atoms in the observable universe is plotted versus the number of protons in the atom[8]. Notice how the abundance of atoms decreases

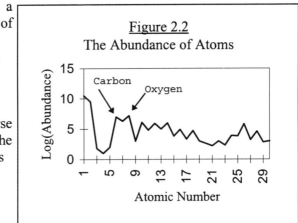

substantially as the number of protons in the atom increases. Then suddenly there is a double-peaked increase in abundance. These two peaks represent the abundances of *carbon and oxygen*. After this peak, the abundance of atoms begin a shaky but steady decrease as the number of protons in the atom increases. Isn't this an incredible coincidence? There just happens to be a peak in the abundance of the two chemicals that must exist in plentiful supply to make life possible. Scientists understand *why* carbon and oxygen are available in such unusually large abundances, and the explanation is fascinating. In order to form a carbon atom, the nuclei (plural of nucleus) of 3 helium atoms must collide and stick. If a fourth helium nucleus were to collide with the carbon, oxygen would result. If only 2 helium nuclei were to collide, a beryllium atom would result. It turns out that the energy of the carbon atom, relative to the other two, is perfectly balanced to ensure that the *most likely atom to be formed from helium collisions is carbon*. In fact, the beryllium atom that is formed when 2 helium nuclei collide is not at all stable. It

15

immediately splits up into two helium atoms again.[9]   If the relative energies of these three atoms were off by as little as 4%, there would not be enough carbon atoms in the entire universe to allow life to exist![10] Once again, it seems almost impossible to assume that such a delicate balance could exist in nature simply by chance.

Of course, a large abundance of carbon is a necessary condition for the formation of life, but it is, by far, not the only condition. The carbon atoms must then bond to other atoms and form all of the molecules that work together to make life possible. Some of these molecules are incredibly complex, and it is hard to believe that they could come about by chance. For example, some of the most important life-giving molecules in nature are called proteins. Proteins are produced in the cells of a living organism, and the proteins that a cell produces determines that cell's function. If a cell produces one set of proteins, it is a skin cell. If it produces another set of proteins, its is a brain cell. Thus, proteins are some of the most important molecules in the chemistry of life.

Proteins are formed when smaller molecules, known as amino acids, link up together in very precise orders. There are 20 different types of amino acids that are found in the proteins necessary for life. The type of amino acids that bond together and the order in which they link up determines the structure and function of the protein. Some rather simple proteins have only 100 or so amino acids linked together. Others have up to 10,000! All of these amino acids must link together in precisely the correct order, or the protein will be absolutely useless. For example, the figure on the next page is a symbolic representation of one of the simplest proteins found in human beings, ribonuclease:[11]

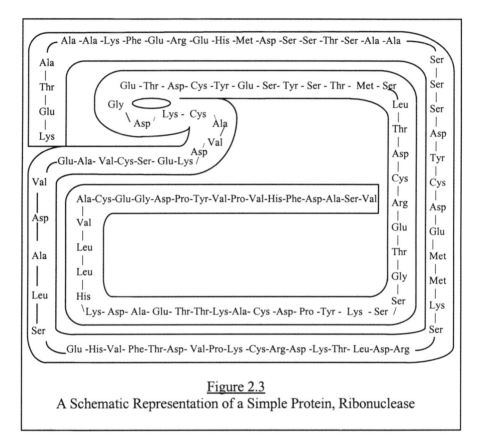

Figure 2.3
A Schematic Representation of a Simple Protein, Ribonuclease

Each three-letter abbreviation in the diagram represents a specific type of amino acid. For example, "Lys" stands for the amino acid Lysine, whereas "Glu" represents the amino acid Glutamic Acid. Ribonuclease contains 17 different types of amino acids linked together 124 times in a very specific order. When assembled in this way, these 124 amino acids form a molecule that performs a vital task in body chemistry. If the amino acids were to link up in the wrong order, or if even one of the amino acids were the wrong type, then ribonuclease would be *completely unable* to perform its job. Thus, if the first amino acid were "Glu" instead of "Lys," the protein would no longer be ribonuclease and would be completely useless. Think, for a moment, about the probability of such a protein forming by chance. Is it possible for such a molecule to form by chance from a mixture of lots of amino acids?

Let's make it easy on ourselves and assume that the only amino acids in the mixture are the 17 types needed to make this particular molecule. In fact, there are many types of amino acids that exist naturally on earth, but adding more amino acid types would significantly reduce our chance of forming ribonuclease. So, in order to make the outcome more likely, we will restrict ourselves to using only the 17 different types of amino acids that make up this molecule. Making this assumption, we can say that the possibility of forming a protein that has "Lys" as its first amino acid is 1 in 17. Those aren't bad odds at all. However, the chance of forming a protein with "Lys" as its first amino acid and "Glu" as its second amino acid are 1 in 17 *times* 1 in 17, or 1 in 289. Suddenly the odds are looking less and less favorable.

The probability of forming a protein whose first three amino acids are "Lys," "Glu," and "Thr" in that order are 1 in 17 *times* 1 in 17 *times* 1 in 17, or 1 in 4,913. If you were to complete this calculation, you would find that the odds for making this protein by chance from a mixture of the proper amino acids is approximately 1 in 10^{152} (a 1 followed by 152 zeros). In order to illustrate just how ridiculously low these odds are, the probability for forming ribonuclease by chance is roughly equivalent to the probability of a poker player drawing a royal flush *19 times in a row without exchanging any cards!* Remember, ribonuclease is a relatively simple protein. There are proteins in our bodies that contain more than 10,000 amino acids! Clearly the idea that these proteins could form by chance is absurd.

If it is very unlikely that proteins could ever form by chance, how can cells manufacture them? Well, inside each cell is an instruction book that gives the cell precise directions on how to make each protein. That instruction book is called deoxyribonucleic acid, or DNA. DNA is a wondrously complex molecule that stores all of the information that every cell needs to perform its job. It stores all of its information with a series of four repeating chemical units called nucleotides. Just as the entire English language can be reduced to a series of dots and dashes in Morse code, all of the information needed by the cells is reduced to repeating sequences of nucleotides. When the cell needs to manufacture proteins, it uses a series of chemical processes to read this "Morse code" and translate it into the amino acid sequences necessary for manufacturing the proper proteins.

The incredible thing about DNA is that this single molecule contains all of the information necessary to build and maintain its living organism. Thus, the DNA that is present in a fish contains all of the information necessary to make and maintain that fish. The DNA that exists in every cell of your body holds all of the secrets of how you are made, what you need to eat, how long you need to sleep, and what your body needs to do to repair itself in case of damage. All of this information is stored in one single molecule. To put this in some kind of perspective, human beings are incapable of making a computer that can hold even a small fraction of the information that is contained in DNA!

The amazing thing about DNA is that it not only contains the information necessary to produce life-giving molecules, but that those life-giving molecules do their jobs in the most efficient way. For example, living organisms use special proteins called enzymes to speed up certain chemical reactions that must take place in order to support life. When a chemical is used in this way, it is often called a "catalyst." Chemists have discovered that the enzymes which are manufactured by living organisms according to the information stored in their DNA are, in fact, more efficient than any catalysts that human scientists can design! Indeed, biochemical engineer Dr. Jonathan Dordick of the University of Iowa says, "Man has yet to devise a catalyst that's as [efficient] as an enzyme."[12] If, after 3,000 years of human science and engineering, we cannot make a computer that comes close to the informational capacity of DNA, and neither can we design enzymes that do their jobs as well as the enzymes that DNA helps produce, how can we believe that DNA simply appeared by chance?

For that matter, how can we believe that life simply appeared by chance? In this chapter, we have seen that the smallest, most fundamental building blocks of life are perfectly designed to work with one another. Each proton, neutron, electron, atom, and molecule fit together in a delicately balanced, intricate web of interaction that forms the basis for life as we know it. If even one of these

19

fundamental building blocks were to have slightly different properties, then life would abruptly cease to exist. Given all of these facts, it becomes increasingly obvious that the phenomenon which we call life is clearly beyond the reach of chance.

ENDNOTES

1. This picture is not entirely correct, but it is a reasonably good way to envision an atom. According to quantum mechanics, the electrons do not whirl around the nucleus in specific orbits, they exists in clouds which are called "electron orbitals."

2. Peter J. Nolan, *Fundamentals of College Physics*, William C. Brown:Dubuque, IA, 1993, pp. 964-965

3. In fact, some carbon atoms can have more than 6 neutrons. A chemical element is determined by the number of protons in the atom. Thus, regardless of how many neutrons an atom has, it is a carbon atom if it has 6 protons. Atoms that have the same number of protons but different numbers of neutrons are called isotopes.

4. John D. Barrow and Frank J. Tipler, *The Anthropic Cosmological Principle*, Oxford University Press:New York, NY 1986, p 400.

5. Robert A. Alberty and Robert J. Silbey, *Physical Chemistry*, John Wiley and Sons:New York, NY, pp.382-412.

6. *Ibid,* pp. 413-414.

7. George Greenstein, *The Symbiotic Universe*, William Morrow:New York, NY, 1988, pp. 64-65

8. Claus E. Rolfs and William S. Rodney, *Cauldrons in the Cosmos*, The University of Chicago Press:Chicago, IL 1988, p. 43

9. Norman E. Holden and F. William Walker, *Chart of Nuclides* (reference chart), General Electric:Schenectady, NY 1972.

10. M. A. Corey, *God and the New Cosmology*, Rowman and Littlefield:Lanham, MD, 1993, pp. 89, 90.

11. Michael Denton, *Evolution: A Theory in Crisis*, Adler and Adler:Bethesda, MD 1986, p. 236.

12. Faye Flam, *Science* **265**, p. 471 (1994).

Chapter 3
A Designer World

Of course, all of the clever design features that we've just discussed are totally useless if they occur in an environment that is hostile to life. In fact, the atoms necessary for the formation of life exist on almost every planet in our solar system. However, of all nine planets, life exists only on earth. Why? The reason is quite simple. Of all planets in this solar system, earth is the only one that is capable of supporting life. As we look into the facts behind why this is so, it will become increasingly clear that earth was specifically *designed* to do just that.

One reason that life flourishes on this planet is that its atmosphere contains just the right mixture of gases. As shown in Figure 3.1, the major constituents of earth's atmosphere are nitrogen (which makes up 78% of the atmosphere), oxygen (21%), argon (0.9%), and carbon dioxide (0.03%).[1] Hundreds of other gases make up the remaining 0.07%. Some of these gases (sulfur dioxide, carbon monoxide, and nitrogen monoxide, for example) are poisonous and would be very toxic if they ever made up a significant fraction of the air we breathe. Other gases (ozone, for example) exist in very small quantities but are, nevertheless, essential for life as we know it. For a myriad of reasons, this mixture of gases is almost perfectly suited for the task of supporting life. If any of the constituent gases made up significantly more or less of the atmosphere than they currently do, earth would suddenly become a planet hostile to all living organisms.

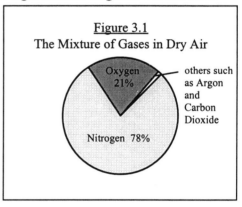

Figure 3.1
The Mixture of Gases in Dry Air

Oxygen 21%

others such as Argon and Carbon Dioxide

Nitrogen 78%

For example, consider the air that you are breathing right now. In order to stay alive, humans and most other forms of life must take in oxygen. This is because the chemical reactions which supply energy for our bodies are combustion reactions. Oxygen is necessary for combustion; thus, most living organisms require a steady supply of it. We are, indeed, fortunate that 21% of the air we breathe is made up of oxygen. If there were significantly less oxygen in the air, we could not supply our bodies with the energy necessary to support their various functions and we would suffocate.

You may not realize, however, that we are also very fortunate that there isn't significantly *more* oxygen in the air, either. If there were significantly more oxygen in the air, then all of the combustion reactions which supply our bodies with energy would speed up. This would result in elevated heart rates, high blood pressure, hyperactivity, and eventually, death. In addition, elevated oxygen content in the earth's atmosphere would result in *significantly* greater risk of natural disaster by fire. For example, the probability that lightning will start a forest fire increases by 70% for every 1% rise in the atmosphere's oxygen content![2] Thus, if oxygen made up 31% of the atmosphere instead of 21%, there would be *seven times more natural forest fires* than there are today.

So we see that although the air we breathe must contain oxygen, it cannot contain very much oxygen. The oxygen has to be "diluted" to exactly the right concentration for healthy lives and safe surroundings. It turns out that the gases used to dilute the oxygen in the air are very important as well. Nitrogen and argon, for example, make up the vast majority of the rest of the air we breathe. These gases are relatively inert. In other words, it is very difficult to get them to chemically react with anything else. Thus, when we breathe in nitrogen and argon, neither of them react with our bodies in any way. We simply breathe them in, and we breathe them right back out again. Its a very nice coincidence that the principle gases used to dilute the oxygen in the atmosphere are two of the very few gases that do not react with our bodies in any way!

In addition to nitrogen, oxygen, and argon, there is a small amount of carbon dioxide in the air. This gas is necessary for life as we know it, but too much carbon dioxide is just as deadly as too little. Carbon dioxide performs two major functions for the maintenance of life on this planet. First, in addition to oxygen, plants need a steady supply of carbon dioxide in order to survive. Through a process called photosynthesis, plants convert the carbon dioxide they absorb from the air and the water they absorb from the ground into glucose, a sugar. This sugar is used by the plant to provide the energy necessary to sustain its life functions.

Photosynthesis not only produces glucose. It also makes oxygen as a byproduct, which is then released into the atmosphere. This replenishes the oxygen supply which is continually used by living organisms. Without carbon dioxide, plants would starve and the oxygen content of the atmosphere would slowly decrease to zero.

In addition to providing the means by which plants can synthesize their own food, carbon dioxide also performs another vital function: it regulates the temperature of the earth. The earth's main source of energy is the sun. Every day, the sun bathes the earth with its light. The earth absorbs most of that light and uses it as a source of energy to grow plants, warm the surface of the planet, etc. Interestingly enough, the earth also radiates energy back into space in the form of infrared light. In fact, the earth radiates a significantly large amount of light. If that were the end of the story, then the earth would be a very, very cold place[3], far too frigid to support life as we know it.

The reason that the earth is not an arctic wasteland is that carbon dioxide (and other gases) tend to absorb some of the light that the earth radiates. This, in turn, heats up the atmosphere, regulating the earth's temperature to near perfect conditions for the maintenance of life. This process is known as the "greenhouse effect."

If the carbon dioxide concentration in the atmosphere were significantly lower, then the earth would be colder. In addition, plants would not be able to manufacture enough food via photosynthesis. If the amount of carbon dioxide in the atmosphere were much greater, then the greenhouse effect would warm the earth up too much, turning much of the world into desert wastelands. This is what some environmentalists have termed "global warming." Although it's debatable whether or not global warming is occurring right now[4-6], it is clear that too much carbon dioxide in the atmosphere would certainly result in a planet that is far too hot to support life.

Oxygen and carbon dioxide are not the only gases that play a critical role in supporting life on earth. Life could not exist at all if it weren't for another gas called ozone. As I've mentioned already, the sun provides the earth with almost all of the energy necessary to support life. Thus, the light that comes from the sun is a necessary ingredient for the maintenance of life on earth. Some of the light that comes from the sun, however, is harmful to living organisms. This light is called ultraviolet light, and it is not visible to the human eye.

Ultraviolet light has so much energy that it kills living tissue. If a living organism is exposed to too much ultraviolet light, its cells will die at a very high rate. If the cells are killed by the ultraviolet light faster than the organism can replace them, the organism will die. If the exposure is not too great, the organism might be able to survive, but its increased rate of cellular production might result in various forms of cancer. Thus, in order to support life, the earth must somehow filter out the dangerous, ultraviolet light while still allowing the rest of the light from the sun (visible and infrared light) to reach its surface.

If you think about it for a minute, filtering light is not an easy task. For example, almost everyone has a filter that they place in their furnace. The purpose of this filter is to remove dust from the air in your house. If the filter were really efficient, there would be so little dust in the air that you would never need to dust your furniture. In fact, these furnace dust filters are usually very inefficient and the result is that we must continually pick up the dust that the filter allows to pass. The reason that some dust passes through the filter is simple: dust particles can be smaller than the holes in the filter. Now, think about this: light has neither size nor mass. It is pure energy. How in the world is the earth able to filter out something that has neither size nor mass?

Ozone, a molecule composed of three oxygen atoms, makes up this amazing filter. It turns out that ozone is a molecule which breaks down in the presence of ultraviolet light. The ultraviolet light has just enough energy to break apart one of the bonds that holds the oxygen atoms together. The bond, in order to break, must absorb the ultraviolet light. In other words, when ultraviolet light encounters an ozone molecule, it uses its energy to destroy the ozone molecule instead of destroying living tissue. One truly incredible thing about this wonderful filter is that ozone cannot be broken down by visible or infrared light, so those types of light are allowed to hit the surface of the earth, where they are needed by plants and animals![7]

That's not the end of the story, however. Because each ozone molecule is destroyed when it absorbs ultraviolet light, there must be some way of replenishing the earth's supply of ozone so that the filtering system will stay intact. This is accomplished through a system of four chemical reactions called the "Chapman cycle." Although the Chapman cycle is far too complicated for the purpose of this discussion, suffice it to say that the earth is continually producing more ozone from its supply of oxygen. Thus, not only is there an elegant filtering system that protects us from the sun's harmful rays, but the earth also has a system that ensures the constant renewal of the filter.[8]

The most amazing aspect of the ozone filter hasn't even been presented yet! Although ozone is necessary for life as we know it, ozone is also incredibly poisonous to living organisms. If living organisms breathe in too much ozone, they die. So, we must have ozone to protect us from the sun's ultraviolet rays, but we cannot breathe it in or it would kill us. Seems like a contradiction, doesn't it? Well it would be, except the *Designer* of our planet is a little smarter than you and me.

Earth's atmosphere contains plenty of ozone, but the vast majority of it exists in a layer of the atmosphere ("the ozone layer") 20 to 30 kilometers (12.4 to 18.6 miles) above sea level, where no living organism breathes![9] Think about all of this for a moment. Earth just *happens* to have all of the gases necessary for life, it just *happens* to have all the right quantities of those gases, and they just *happen* to be in the right place. All of this is incredible enough, but there is a lot more to the earth than its atmosphere! For example, let's think about all of the energy that is coming to the earth from the sun.

Although energy is a very good thing, its possible to have too much of a good thing. Thus, if a planet is to support life, it must have an adequate supply of energy but, at the same time, not too much. What determines the amount of energy that the earth gets from the sun? Well, there are (once again) several interdependent processes that regulate earth's energy inventory, but the most important consideration is, simply, earth's distance away from the sun.

The earth orbits around the sun in a nearly circular pattern, thus, it stays at an almost constant distance away from the sun. If that distance were to change by as little as 2%, there would be disastrous consequences! In order for life as we know it to exist, the water on the planet must be stable in its liquid phase (as opposed to its solid phase, ice, or its gaseous phase, vapor). If earth were 2% farther away from or closer to the sun, there would not be enough liquid water on the planet to support any kind of life![10]

Lets look at another aspect of our designer planet, shall we? The earth not only orbits around the sun, but it also rotates on its own vertical axis. Whereas the earth's orbit around the sun is the cause of the changing seasons, the earth's rotation around its vertical axis is responsible for changing night into day and vice-versa. What you may not realize, however, is that the earth's vertical axis is not positioned straight up and down. It tilts to one side just a bit. That is why most globes that you see are, themselves, tilted. They mimic what the earth really looks like as it spins in space. You may not believe it, but this tilt is just one more little feature that makes life possible here on earth.

Because the earth tilts, it exposes a larger fraction of its surface to the sun than it would otherwise. This exposure helps regulate the surface temperature of the planet, by making sure that no part of the earth is shielded from the sun's light for an inordinate amount of time. The earth's present tilt exposes the largest amount of surface area to the sun's light at any one time. If the tilt were greater or less, even by just a small amount, surface temperatures on the earth would be too extreme to support life.[11]

Not only is the earth's axial tilt important for the existence of life, but the speed at which it rotates about that axis is equally important. It takes 24 hours for the earth to make one full rotation on its axis, and that's why a day is 24 hours long. If the earth's rotation were significantly faster, then winds on the planet would regularly reach hurricane velocity. If, instead, the rotation speed of the earth were significantly slower, then the difference between daytime and nighttime temperatures would become too extreme to support life.[12]

Earth is also equipped with a magnetic field. This is what causes the Boy Scout compass to point north. It is used by people (and a few animals) to navigate around the globe, but it is also absolutely necessary for life as we know it. The earth is constantly being bombarded by cosmic radiation. This radiation is not blocked by the ozone layer and would be deadly to life if it were allowed to reach earth's surface. It's the magnetic field that keeps these harmful particles away from the surface of the earth and allows life to exist.[13]

Are you beginning to get the picture? Earth is an incredibly complex system of interacting processes that all work together to make this planet a haven for life. If any one of these processes were to stop working, then life would abruptly come to an end. Incredibly, the features that I have discussed represent only a small fraction of all of the wonderful features that make earth habitable for life.

In fact, Hugh Ross has listed an additional 24 features which allow earth to support life in his book, *The Creator and The Cosmos.*[14] Using these facts, Dr. Ross (conservatively) estimates that the probability of a planet like earth forming by chance is approximately 1 in 10^{42} (a 1 followed by 42 zeros).[15] Once again, this is a ridiculously absurd probability. You've heard about the improbability of finding a needle in a haystack? Well, the bigger the haystack, the more improbable it will be to find the needle, right? If you were to cover the entire earth with hay and stack it all of the way to the moon, you would still be more likely to reach once into that haystack and pull out the needle than for the earth to have been formed by chance! Clearly, then, the idea that the earth could simply exist as a result of blind chance is ludicrous in the highest degree!

ENDNOTES

1. *Chemistry in Context*, American Chemical Society, William C. Brown:Dubuque, IA, 1994, p. 7. (These numbers assume that the air is dry, i.e., that humidity is zero.)

2. Barrow, John D. and Tipler, Frank J., *The Anthropic Cosmological Principle*, Oxford University Press:Oxford, 1986, p. 544

3. *Chemistry in Context*, p. 64.

4. Albert Gore, *Earth in the Balance: Ecology and the Human Spirit*, Houghton Mifflin:Boston, MA 1992.

5. Ronald Bailey, *Ecoscam: The False Prophets of the Ecological Apocalypse*, St. Martin's Press:New York, NY 1993.

6. Dixy Lee Ray and Lou Guzzo, *Environmental Overkill Whatever Happened to Common Sense?*, Regnery Gateway:Washington, DC 1993.

7. *Chemistry in Context*, pp. 39-40.

8. *Ibid*, pp. 42-43.

9. *Ibid*, p. 6.

10. Michael H. Hart, *Icharus* **37**, pp.351-357 (1979).

11. Hugh Ross, *The Fingerprint of God*, Promise Publishing:Orange, CA, 1990, p. 130

12. *Ibid.*

13. P. C. W. Davies, *Other Worlds*, Simon and Schuster:New York, NY, 1980, p. 43.

14. Hugh Ross, *The Creator and the Cosmos,* Navpress:Colorado Springs, CO, 1993.

15. *Ibid,* pp. 129-132.

Chapter 4
Life Itself

So far, we've seen that the chemistry, physics, and structural makeup of the earth is perfectly suited for life. Now let's examine life itself. Is life something that can just appear by chance? Is it really possible that random chemical reactions, acting over millions or perhaps billions of years, could produce a living system? Well, let's examine the nature and structure of life, and see if such an event is scientifically feasible.

Just as matter has fundamental building blocks called atoms, life has fundamental building blocks called "cells." Some living organisms are composed of only one cell. Bacteria, amoebae, and certain forms of algae are examples of such single-celled life forms. Most living creatures, however, are multi-cellular life forms, being composed of a huge number of cells that work together to make sure the organism survives. Since a multi-celled life form must have cells that not only work on their own but also work together, single-celled life forms are usually considered to be the simplest known forms of life.

Let's examine a single cell and see how simple it really is. Figure 4.1 is a simple, idealized, schematic diagram of a typical animal cell. Most kinds of animal life will be made up of one or more cells which strongly resemble the diagram of Figure 4.1 shown on the next page. The first thing you will notice about the animal cell in the picture is that it contains many different components. Just like the components of a watch, the components of a cell all work together and are finely tuned to one another to ensure proper function of the cell.

Each component of the cell has its job to do. If, for some reason, one of the components ceases to do its job or ceases to communicate with the other components in the cell, the cell will die. In order to show you just how complicated the *simplest* version of life is, let me (in brief) explain the main functions of some of the cellular components shown in Figure 4.1.

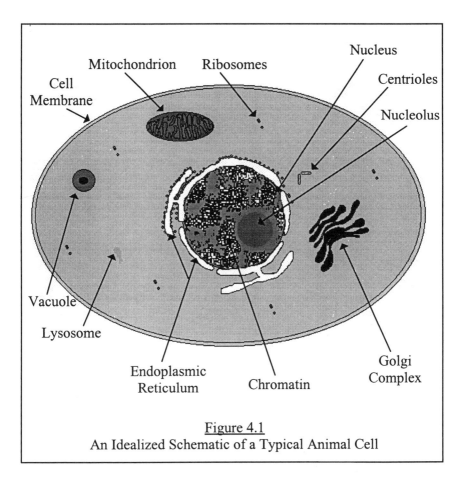

Figure 4.1
An Idealized Schematic of a Typical Animal Cell

One thing that you will quickly notice about the cell in Figure 4.1 is that it is surrounded by a membrane. The membrane is a necessary component of the cell, because the cell is filled with a jelly-like substance known as cytoplasm. This cytoplasm must be held within the cell by the membrane. At the same time, however, the membrane must allow nutrients, water, and oxygen to enter the cell so as to support the chemical reactions necessary for life. Because this membrane allows certain things to pass through (nutrients, water, and oxygen) while not allowing other things to pass through (cytoplasm, toxins, and cellular components), it is called "semipermeable."

Once the semipermeable membrane allows nutrients, water, and oxygen into the cell, they are transported to the places that they are needed. Water is sent principally to the lysosome where it is used in chemical reactions that break down complex nutrients into simple sugars. These simple sugars are transported to the mitochondria where they are burned (chemically reacted with oxygen) to produce energy. The ribosomes produce proteins using the energy supplied by the mitochondria, chemicals supplied by the lysosome, and a blueprint provided by the DNA (Chromatin) in the nucleus. Nucleoli help in copying the DNA blueprint for this process. In order to ensure continuous function, the Golgi complex stores excess nutrients for future use. Any waste products are sent out of the cell by vacuoles. The Centriole aid in reproduction.

The point to this entire discussion is that the cell represented in Figure 4.1 is one of the *simplest* versions of life.[1] Clearly this wonderful system is far more complicated than a watch. Nevertheless, whereas no one would ever make the absurd assumption that a watch could simply appear by chance, many scientists want to convince you and me that this infinitely more complicated mechanism did just that.

Once again, of course, evolutionists will try to convince you that the cells we see today are actually far more complicated than the cells that first appeared on earth. Evolutionists believe that the first type of cell to appear on earth was something called a "protocell." These protocells were much, much simpler than the cells we see today. Since protocells are relatively simple, these scientists say, then its not so unlikely that they could have appeared by chance. Once these "simple" protocells appeared, then, they could slowly evolve into the more complicated cells that we see today, being guided by thousands of millions of years of natural selection.

Now, on face value, such an explanation might be attractive. However, when one begins to look at this explanation with a somewhat critical eye, the whole scenario begins to dissolve in a mist of improbability and assumption. First of all, we've never seen a protocell.[2] We have no idea what one might even look like. This whole business of protocells, then, is simply one big assumption. Of course, assumptions are not necessarily bad in scientific inquiry. All scientists must make assumptions about the nature of what they are

34

trying to study. The point is, however, that the assumption must be believable. Since evolutionists are forced to assume that protocells once existed, we must see how believable such an assumption is.

In order to examine this assumption, we must first see what evolutionists assume that a protocell should be capable of. The minimum requirements for life, according to experts in origin of life research[3], are as follows:

> 1. Protocells must have the equivalent of a semipermeable membrane that allows nutrients to pass through while keeping the inner constituents of the cell from leaking out of the cell and toxins from coming into the cell.

> 2. The semipermeable membrane must be able to change to allow for cellular growth.

> 3. Protocells must have a mechanism that will allow the transport of nutrients from the environment to the inner parts of the protocell.

> 4. Protocells must have a system for producing proteins that can be used to build, grow, and repair cellular components as well as to allow for reproduction.

> 5. Protocells must have chemical mechanisms established that will convert nutrients into energy.

According to the experts, these are the *minimum* requirements necessary for a chemical system to be considered a "living" cell. Think about it for a minute. These five characteristics describe an incredibly complicated system. The semipermeable membrane alone is a marvelous feat of chemical technology. In order to be semipermeable, the membrane must be able to recognize what molecules to let in and what molecules to keep out. It's not a simple filter, because some molecules that cells need are quite big, whereas some poisonous molecules are quite small. If the membrane were to keep out big molecules and let small ones in like a normal filter, important nutrients would never enter the cell, but some poisons would. Thus, the semipermeable membrane must have complicated chemical mechanisms by which it can distinguish "good molecules" from "bad molecules."

Each one of the five characteristics listed must be supported by complex webs of chemical reactions each communicating with and supporting the others. If just one of these chemical reactions stops working, then the cell stops living. Clearly this is still more complicated than a watch. If it is self-evident that a watch cannot simply form by chance, then it is self-evident that even "simple" life forms cannot appear by chance.

Remember, the theory of evolution by natural selection is of no help in forming the first living cell, because the theory of evolution *assumes* that we are dealing with a living system. The ideas of competition, fitness to survive, and variation in reproduction do not make any sense except in the context of a living system; thus, we cannot use the concept of slow gradual change guided by natural selection to explain the appearance of life. In order for life to appear by chance, all of the necessary components would have to miraculously come together at once, in exactly the same way that our watch would appear instantaneously if all of the elements in the desert were to collide together in one, big, happy coincidence.

Of course, there are many well-respected scientists[4] who disagree with the above argument. Some, in fact, feel that it is obvious[5] that life can appear by chance. These scientists have never given any experimental or theoretical justification for their views, nevertheless, they strongly cling to the fervent belief that life can spontaneously create itself. For people such as this, an even greater mystery needs to be explained: how could evolution ever produce some of the elegantly designed life forms that we see today? When a scientist begins to study the world around him, he will find creatures whose biological functions not only defy the theory of evolution but also provide even further evidence for a designer. These life forms will be discussed in the next chapter.

ENDNOTES

1. There is another type of single-celled life that may be simpler than that shown in Figure 4.1. There is a class of cells known as "prokaryotic cells." These cells are often considered the simplest form of life because paleontologists believe that they were the first form of life to populate the earth and because they do not have all of the individual components shown in the figure. These cells perform all of the functions of life without having separate components to perform the individual tasks. Although evolutionists often assume that prokaryotic cells are simpler than the type of cell (eukaryotic cell) shown in Figure 4.1, its not clear that this assumption is valid. Since prokaryotic cells do perform essentially all of the same functions of eukaryotic cells, how can they be any simpler? They may *look* simpler, but it's not clear that they *are* simpler.

2. Once again, some evolutionists think that prokaryotic cells might, indeed, be examples of protocells. However, as was pointed out in the first note, it's not clear that prokaryotic cells are any less complicated than eukaryotic cells, so there is no real evidence to back up such a claim.

3. D. W. Deamer and G. R. Fleischaker, in *Origin of Life, The Central Concepts*, Jones and Bartlett:Boston, MA 1994, pp. 227-231

4. *Ibid.*

5. P. W. Atkins, *Creation Revisited*, W. H. Freeman and Co.:New York, NY, 1992.

Chapter 5
Elegance and Beauty in Nature

As mentioned previously, one of the best ways of refuting the theory of evolution is to examine the beautiful, elegantly designed creatures that inhabit planet earth. Their existence cannot be understood within the framework of evolutionary theory. For example, consider the case of the bombardier beetle[1]. This ugly little beetle has one of the most beautiful defense mechanisms in all of creation: a fully-equipped chemical weapon.

This weapon begins with storage vessels that contain a mixture of two chemicals: hydroquinone and hydrogen peroxide. Under normal conditions, these chemicals would react but, while stored in the bombardier beetle's vessels, they are kept from reacting by the presence of a third chemical which inhibits the reaction. When the bombardier beetle feels threatened, however, it fills an empty reaction chamber in its body with the chemicals. Two other chemicals, catalase and peroxidase, are then added. These chemicals cause the hydrogen peroxide and hydroquinone to react violently. The violent reaction produces a great amount of heat and pressure in the reaction vessel. The beetle then points its tail in the direction of trouble, and opens a valve that exists between the reaction vessel and the tail. A jet of steam which has a temperature of roughly 200°F shoots out the tail in the direction of danger.[2] Any potential predator is immediately burned and frightened away! The bombardier beetle can perform this feat up to twenty times per day!

Now think about this incredibly elegant defense mechanism for a minute. This is a fully-functional chemical weapon. Human beings, with all of our technological knowledge and research genius were only able to develop effective chemical weapons during World War I, but the simple bombardier beetle has had such a device since day one! Does it make any sense at all to believe that something which took centuries of human research and development could have simply appeared by chance in the body of a beetle?

In addition, think how an evolutionist would have to explain the development of such a defense mechanism. He would start by assuming that there was some form of beetle with no such defense mechanism. As time went on, however, the individual parts of the defense mechanism would appear one by one. Perhaps in the first generation the storage vessels would appear. Then, a few generations later, the beetle would develop the ability to manufacture one or two of the five chemicals necessary for the weapon. As more and more generations of beetles followed, eventually the beetles would develop the ability to produce all five of the necessary chemicals. Then, perhaps, the reaction vessel would develop, conveniently linked to the storage vessels. Finally, the valve between the tail and the reaction vessel would develop, and the weapon would be fully functional.

This little fantasy might seem plausible until we remember the principle tenant of evolutionary theory: natural selection. If a beetle was born that had only one, two, or even three of the components necessary for the weapon, then that beetle would not be any more likely to survive than a beetle with none of the components. Unless the chemical weapon was fully functional, it would provide no survival advantage to the beetle. Thus, if a beetle was born with only a few of the weapon's components, there is no reason to believe that it would survive in order to pass on these traits to its offspring. So, in order for this weapon to have evolved, it must have appeared, fully functional, in one and only one generation. This, of course, is ludicrous; therefore, the theory of evolution by natural selection is hopelessly inadequate at explaining the existence of this marvelous creature.

If the bombardier beetle were the only life form that had such elegantly designed characteristics, then perhaps the theory of evolution would not be in such trouble. However, as we look around this incredible creation that God has given us, we can see many, many more examples of design that provide evidence for His handiwork.

The feeding habits of the shark also defy description from an evolutionary standpoint. Many species of shark enjoy eating flounder, a flat fish whose colorings often match the sand at the bottom of the ocean. When a flounder lies motionless at the bottom of the sea, it is almost impossible to distinguish it from the sand. Nevertheless, when a shark passes near a flounder, the shark will immediately dive and bite the sand. Unerringly, the shark will end up with a flounder in its mouth. How does it do that? How does the shark know that a flounder is resting on the ocean bottom, despite the fact that it is so well hidden?

Most people, when faced with such a question, might guess that the shark smells the flounder, feels the vibrations which the flounder makes when it moves, or perhaps just has very keen eyesight. All of those guesses make sense, but they are also wrong. In order to detect the presence of a flounder at the bottom of the ocean, a shark relies on its amazing three-dimensional electric field sensor.[3] This electric field sensor is precisely tuned to detect the voltages that are associated with the electrochemical reactions which control the flounder's muscles. Its precision is estimated to be equal to 0.00000005 volts per centimeter. To illustrate just what that means: if the army were to make such an electric field sensor, it would be capable of pinpointing the precise location of a transistor radio battery 1,118 miles away! To this day, modern science and technology has not been able to develop an electric field sensor with anywhere near that kind of precision.

Of course, the first thing that an evolutionist would like you to believe is that a device which modern-day science cannot match in precision was developed in the shark by blind chance. That assertion is silly enough. However, when we examine the development of the shark's feeding habits from an evolutionary perspective, we are once again completely confounded. After all, the shark has an incredibly complex method of finding its prey. Why would evolution develop such an intricate prey detection mechanism if other, simpler mechanisms are at hand? Why didn't sharks simply evolve with keener eyesight or a heightened sense of smell? Those answers to the shark's feeding needs would have been much more likely in an evolutionary framework. Also, this complicated system would have clearly taken a long, long time to develop. How did the sharks find prey while this more complex system was being developed? Why, if they could find prey over this extended period of time, would another method for finding prey develop? Such questions cannot be adequately answered in the context of evolution.

Let's consider something a little more close to home now: the human eye. The human eye is probably the most complicated organ in all of nature. It is so incredibly complex in its design that Charles Darwin, in his book *Origin of the Species*, said:

To suppose that the eye, with all its inimitable contrivances for adjusting the focus to different distances, for admitting different amounts of light, and for the correction of spherical and chromatic aberration, could have been formed by natural selection, seems, I freely confess, absurd in the highest degree.[4]

So we see that Charles Darwin himself agrees that his theory is hopelessly inadequate for explaining the existence of complex organs and organisms in nature. What is truly incredible about Darwin's admission is that we now know that the eye is significantly more complex than was ever imagined in his day!

Another interesting fact about the eye which defies the theory of evolution is the composition of its tears. During normal operation, the eye is constantly being bathed in tears which are emitted by sponge-like glands that rest above the eye in the eye socket. These tears are composed mostly of salt, water, and lysozyme[5]. The saltwater tends to lubricate the eye and the lysozyme is an antibacterial agent which fights eye infections. The tears cover the eye and then drain away through the *lacrimal punctum*. When the human eye gets irritated by the presence of a foreign object, its tear glands emit more tears than the *lacrimal punctum* can drain away. These excess tears tend to flow out of the eye, washing out the foreign object and soothing the eye. When we see tears flowing out of a person's eye, we say that the person is crying.

Of course, human eyes also release excess tears in response to strong emotional feelings, i.e., when we are sad, we cry. Amazingly enough, the tears that we cry when our eyes are irritated are chemically quite different from the tears we cry when we are upset! Tears produced by strong emotions contain chemicals that do not appear (to any great extent) in tears produced by eye irritants. These chemicals include manganese (a chemical depressant), leucine-enkephalin (an endorphin which helps control pain), and the adrenocorticotrophic hormone (a hormone produced by bodies under stress).[6-7] When you excrete these chemicals by crying, the net effect is to *make you feel better*. By releasing these toxins, the tears serve to chemically and physically make the crier feel less depressed!

Since humans are the only animal species that can cry as a result of emotion, then the evolutionist is forced to assume that this property of human tears evolved in only the human race over a long time period. Think about it for a minute, though. What possible survival advantage is obtained by feeling better as a result of a good cry? The answer, of course, is none whatsoever. In fact, those who bottle up their emotions are usually more aggressive, which, according to evolutionary principles, should make them more fit to battle for survival. Thus, if anything, this particular feature of human chemistry is harmful to the species' ability to survive and would be thrown out by natural selection. According to evolutionary theory, then, this trait should *never have evolved.* If, instead, we view the human body as a marvelously designed organic machine, we can assume that the tears we shed are a gift from the designer. Since He built in us the ability for emotions, He also built in us the ability to deal with those emotions. One of those is the ability to sit down and have a good, long cry.

Finally, there is one other aspect of nature for which evolutionary theory can never hope to offer substantial explanation: symbiosis. Symbiosis is the name given to describe a situation in which two or more life forms work together to ensure each other's survival. There are literally thousands of examples of symbiosis in nature, some very simple and some very complex. Although evolutionary theory has some hope of explaining the simple instances of symbiosis, the more complex forms of this phenomenon can never be fit into an evolutionary framework. We will concentrate on a particularly startling example: the case of the Oriental sweetlips and the blue-streak wrasse.[8]

The Oriental sweetlips is a species of fish that has teeth. Teeth are rare in underwater life, but there are forms of fish that must have them in order to be able to balance the underwater ecosystem. Some forms of underwater life would not have predators unless other species of fish possessed teeth. The problem with teeth, however, is that they must be cleaned or they will eventually rot away. Humans, of course, clean their teeth with toothpaste and toothbrushes. How do other species clean their teeth? Usually they do so by chewing on hard, edible substances. Dogs, for example, chew on bones. The hard bones tend to chip away at the plaque buildup on dogs' teeth, effectively cleaning them.

Underwater, unfortunately, there are not a lot of hard, edible substances. Thus, if the Oriental sweetlips has teeth, it must find an alternative method to clean them. The way it does this is quite remarkable. After swimming around all day, feeding on little fish, the Oriental sweetlips decides that it is time to have its teeth cleaned.

In order to accomplish this, the sweetlips begins to look for a particular color of coral. When it finds that coral, it swims up, opens it mouth, and waits. Soon, several small fish (blue-streak wrasses) dart from the coral reef and *swim directly into the open mouth of the sweetlips.* The wrasses then begin to eat the food buildup that has developed on the sweetlips' teeth. Once the wrasses have finished, the sweetlips allows them to leave so that they can clean another sweetlips' teeth.

Think about this incredible relationship for a moment. The sweetlips could not survive without the help of the wrasse. Neither could the wrasse exist without the sweetlips. Additionally, remember that the sweetlips spends its whole day eating other little fish. Somehow, however, the sweetlips knows not to eat this particular little fish. In the same way, the wrasse spend its whole day hiding from bigger fish. It somehow knows, however, not to be afraid of this particular big fish. It somehow knows to swim straight into the jaws of death without any fear at all!

Think for a minute how an evolutionist would attempt to explain this complex relationship. At some point in time, the sweetlips' ancestors had no teeth. In a number of generations, however, teeth began to form in a few of the ancestor's offspring. Now, in order for these teeth to avoid falling out, this new fish would have to develop the instinct for seeking out the wrasse and not eating it. This instinct, of course, would have to evolve *at exactly the same time* that the sweetlips' teeth evolved. That's not enough, however. *At the exactly same time that the teeth and instincts evolved in the sweetlips, the wrasse would have to develop the instinct to swim right into the sweetlips' mouth without fear of being eaten!* Remember, if all of these things didn't happen in the same exact generation, then the system would not work.

Once again, this entire situation is impossible to explain from an evolutionary point of view. Obviously it is ridiculous to believe in all of these chance coincidences occurring all at the same time. Over and over again, however, this is what the scientist who is unwilling to believe in God *must* believe. When one, as a scientist, begins to look at the world around him, he sees far too many of these "happy coincidences." Between all of the precisely balanced properties of atoms and subatomic particles, the incredibly complex web of interactions that make life on earth possible, the complicated nature of life itself, and the amazing design features of the animals we see in the world around us, it becomes intuitively obvious that this fantastic world around us could never have appeared by chance. It must have been designed by a powerful and intelligent designer. As Sir Frederick Hoyle (arguably England's foremost astrophysicist) says,

> ...A common sense interpretation of the facts suggests that a superintellect has monkeyed with physics, as well as with chemistry and biology, and that there are no blind forces worth speaking about in nature. The numbers one calculates from the facts seem to me so overwhelming as to put this conclusion almost beyond question.[5]

It is this "superintellect," this "intelligent designer," that Christians call God.

ENDNOTES

1. T. Eisner and D. J. Aneshansky, *Science*, **215**, p. 83 (1982).

2. Duane T. Gish, *Creation Scientists Answer Their Critics*, Institute for Creation Research: El Cajon, 1993 , pp. 101, 102.

3. A. Kalmijn, *Science*, **218**, p. 916 (1982).

4. Charles Darwin, *The Origin of the Species*, Penguin Classics:London, 1985, p. 217.

5. Ashley Montague, *Science Digest*, November , p. 32 (1981).

6. Gregg Levoy, *Psychology Today*, July/August, pp. 8-10 (1988).

7. Lael Wertenbaker, *The Eye: Window to the World*, Torstar Books:New York, NY, 1984.

8. Robert Doolan, *Creation Ex Nihilo* **15.4**, pp. 28-29 (1993).

9. Fred Hoyle, *Engineering and Science* November, 1981, p. 8-12.

Chapter 6
Head and Shoulders Above the Rest

Once the rational person has seen the convincing way that scientific fact supports the existence of a Creator, a very important question should spring to mind. Who is this Creator? If we are to call Him "God," what is His nature? Is He an aloof, uncaring God who simply started life on its way and then sat back to watch? Is He a capricious being who creates and destroys on the basis of whim? Is He a loving, caring God who is deeply involved in every aspect of His creation?

Of course, it will be very difficult to rely solely upon science to answer these important questions. After all, science certainly cannot describe the nature of something which is, by definition, supernatural. Although science provides strong evidence that God exists, it cannot determine much about His nature or personality. The rational person is not without help, however. Throughout the course of human history, thousands of books have been written which attempt to answer these very questions. From the ruminations of Socrates to the rantings of Adolf Hitler, the literature of humanity is full of works which claim to know the mind of God.

With all of these works at his disposal, the rational person can surely find out something concerning this being which he calls "God." Of course, the first thing he must do is find some means of sorting through the various works which claim to reveal the nature of God. Not only would it be impossible for one person to read and understand all of humanity's works concerning the Creator, it would also be rather pointless. After all, many of the works concerning God contradict one another. The sacred writings of the Hindus (primarily the *Vedas* and the *Upanishads*) say that God is formless and abstract, having no personal attributes. On the other hand, the Islamic scriptures (the *Quran*) say that God is single being with many personal attributes. Things get even more confusing when one compares these views on God to those written in the Bible. According to the Bible, God is a triune being in which each of the three parts embody different aspects of His personal characteristics.

These works not only contradict one another concerning the nature of God, they also contradict one another concerning certain

46

historical details. For example, whereas the Bible states that Christ was crucified on a cross, the Quran states quite clearly that he was not.[1]

Thus, in order to help narrow the field, the rational person must begin looking at those works which seem to "stand out" from the rest. Any book that is clearly unique should be among the first works considered for examination. While looking over the vast sea of human literature, there is certainly one book that stands head and shoulders above the others: the Bible. The Bible is, by far, the most unique book in all of human history.

Consider, for a moment, the **composition** of the Bible. The Bible is a collection of books that were written over the course of more than 1,500 years. What other book can claim to be so timeless?

While most books give the reader a point of view which encompasses one or two generations, the Bible provides insights from more than seventy. If you think that the Bible is outdated, just try to find another work in all of human history that encompasses such a large number of human eras.

The Bible not only encompasses several different generations, it also encompasses all walks of life. The authors who have contributed to the Bible make up a diverse sampling of people from various linguistic traditions, educational experiences, and vocational choices. For example, Luke (the writer of "The Gospel According to Luke" and "The Acts of the Apostles") was a highly educated physician. On the other hand, Peter (the writer of "First Peter " and "Second Peter") was an uneducated fisherman. Moses (the writer of the first five books of the Old Testament) was a celebrated political activist while Nehemiah (the author of "Nehemiah") was a lowly servant. The Bible wasn't even written in a single language. The more than forty authors whose works appear in the Bible wrote in either Hebrew, Aramaic, or Greek. Once again, there is no other book in all of human history which contains such a diverse set of authors!

The Bible is not only unique when in comes to its **composition**, however. It is also unique in its **popularity.** There is no other book in all of human history that is in as much demand as the Bible. For example, as of May 31, 1993, the Gideons International had distributed a total of 597,996,384 copies of either the entire Bible or the New Testament. Of these Scriptures, 383,584,306 were distributed in countries other than the United States.[2] Between the dates of May 31, 1992 and May 31, 1993 alone, the Gideons distributed 38,514,443 copies of Scripture. Clearly, if the Bible were not popular, the Gideons could not distribute so many copies.

Of course, the Gideons are not the only ones who make Scriptures available to people. Even in the 1940's, the British and Foreign Bible Society had to print a copy of the Bible every three seconds, day and night, just to meet its demand.[3] The Christian Booksellers Association in America sells 450 different English versions of the Bible for a currency volume exceeding $400,000,000 per year.[4] As the *Cambridge History of the Bible* says, "No other book has known anything approaching this constant circulation."[5]

The Bible's popularity is evident not only by the fact that it is in demand, but also by how highly regarded it is. According to a survey reported in the *Washington Post*, more than 50% of adult Americans read the Bible monthly.[6] In addition, the *Los Angeles Times* reports that 73% of all Americans believe that it is important to read the Bible.[7] People are also willing to spend a lot of money to get their hands on a Bible. A 1,000 year-old Bible sold in London for a world-record setting price of 3.19 million dollars![8] Data such as these simply illustrate that the Bible is very popular. Every year the Bible outsells all other books available to humanity and is still the most highly regarded work in the world.

Not only is the Bible unique in its **composition** and **popularity,** however, it is also unique in its **survivability**. No other book has been fought against to the extent which the Bible has. From the nearly incomprehensible babble that comes from the intelligentsia of the universities' ivory towers to the venomous attacks leveled by various governments and regimes, the Bible and the Christians who believe in it have been vilified, ridiculed, and even outlawed. Against all odds, however, the Bible still survives. Indeed, as H. L. Hastings has said, "Infidels for eighteen hundred years have been refuting and overthrowing this book, and yet it stands today as solid as a rock."[9]

Even a brief glance at history shows the great extent of persecution through which Christianity and the Bible have survived.

As early as A.D. 64, Nero began persecuting the Christians because he found them a convenient scapegoat for the fire which devastated Rome.[10]   Throughout the next 2.5 centuries, Christians were persecuted by both the Romans and the Jews.   Thousands of Christians were put to death during this time, simply because they believed in the disciples' accounts that told how Jesus Christ rose from the dead.[11]   Then, on February 23, A.D. 303, the Roman Emperor Diocletian issued an edict which outlawed Christianity. The edict stated that churches were to be destroyed, Christian public officials were to be removed from office, and the Christian Scriptures were to be handed over so that they could be burned.[12]   Over the next 8 years while the Roman Empire was trying to carry out Diocletian's edict, it went through six more emperors and joint-emperors.[13]   Finally, the newest[14] Roman Emperor, Constantine I, stopped the persecution of the Christians[15], and, by A.D. 328, had actually ordered 50 new copies of the Christian Scriptures to be prepared at the government's expense![16]   Even the might of the Roman Empire could not destroy the Bible or the spread of the Christian church.

Although Christians and the Bible were never again persecuted as ruthlessly and relentlessly as they were under the Romans, there have always been those who have tried, in one way or another, to destroy the Bible and its believers. For example, in 1778, the famous French author Voltaire said that in one hundred years from his time, Christianity would no longer exist. He felt that the intellectual revolution that was taking place at his time would throw Christianity and the Bible into the dustbin of history. That never happened. Instead, Christianity flourished and Voltaire died, with his works never reaching anything close to the popularity of the Bible. As a matter of fact, only fifty years after his death, the Geneva Bible Society used his printing press in his house to produce thousands of Bibles![17]

In an equally ironic twist of history, *Pravda*, the publisher which produced the Soviet Union's official newspaper, is now printing Bibles! Yes, the same publishing company which regularly printed venomous attacks on the Bible is now printing up to 10 million copies of it for Alexis III, the patriarch of the Russian Orthodox Church![18]   So, we see that even a brief glimpse of history shows that the Bible has weathered more persecution than any other literary work and is still the most popular book in the world!

The Bible is not only unique in its **composition, popularity, and survivability**, however. One of the most important aspects of the Bible is its **influence**. Clearly, the influence that the Bible has had on Western thought, philosophy, civilization, and literature is like no other book in the world. For example, every major university in the Western world has at least one course (usually a series of courses) devoted exclusively to the Bible. There is no other book in the history of humanity that can make that statement. Why is the Bible so extensively studied on university campuses? Because of its unparalleled influence on human thought.

Consider the Bible's influence on human literature. According to Professor T. R. Henn, "To glance at even a fraction of the imagery drawn from Biblical sources would be an impossible task."[19] This is an obvious statement to anyone that has even a rudimentary knowledge of literature. Just think for a moment what Shakespeare's plays, John Donne's poetry, or T.S. Elliot's stories would be like if there were no Bible! Indeed, many literary critics believe that it is impossible to appreciate most of the literature of humanity without first understanding the Bible. As Professor Northrup Frye states, "Once our view of the Bible comes into focus, a great mass of literary symbols...begin to take on meaning."[20]

Perhaps the most accurate statement concerning the influence of the Bible can be drawn from Cleland B. McAfee. In his book, *The Greatest English Classic*, he says,

> If every Bible in any considerable city were destroyed, the Book could be restored in all its essential parts from the quotations on the shelves of the city public library. There are works, covering almost all the great literary writers, devoted especially to showing how much the Bible has influenced them.[21]

Why has the Bible asserted such influence on literature? Simply because it is the *greatest* work of literature in the entire world. As Professor C. A. Dinsmore aptly puts it, "...merely as art, this tremendous drama, this divine human comedy, makes the plot of the *Iliad* or of *Hamlet* seem very insignificant."[22] Its literary merits by themselves make the Bible worth reading and studying by anyone who wants to proclaim himself or herself "educated."

The Bible's influence does not stop at literature, however. The Bible has exerted tremendous influence on our concepts of civilization, law, and society. Consider, for example, the moving words of former President Woodrow Wilson:

> ...not a little of the history of liberty lies in the circumstance that the moving sentences of this Book were made familiar to the ears and the understandings of those people who have led mankind in exhibiting the forms of government and the impulses of reform which have made for freedom and self-government among mankind.[23]

Former President Wilson believed that the Bible itself was the main foundation upon which the United States was built. Indeed, he is not the only one who feels that way. Abraham Katsh, in his book, *The Biblical Heritage of American Democracy*, attributes the United States' Constitution, its concept of individual freedom, its legislative system, and its judicial system to the Bible.[24] If the Bible were never written, the United States of America probably would have never existed! Truly, no other literary work in the world has influenced humanity as significantly as the Bible!

Finally, the Bible is not only unique in its **composition, popularity, survivability, and influence**, but it is also unique in its **central character**, Jesus Christ. Jesus is by far the most important human being to ever walk the face of the earth. Even those who are anti-Christian will nevertheless agree that Christ himself was the best teacher of morality and virtue that this world has ever seen. Not only did His teachings outline the tenets of morality, but His life illustrated them.

Christ was more than just a teacher, however. He was a man who claimed to be the Messiah. Although such a claim is pretty astounding, it was not all that uncommon during Jesus' time. The people of Israel were so tired of Rome's tyranny, that anyone who promised to overthrow the Empire was followed by more than a handful of people.

One example of a would-be messiah was Judah the Macabee, an early Jewish opponent of Assyria. In 168 BC, the Emperor,

Antiochus Epiphanes, outlawed Judaism and its customs and erected a statue of Zeus in the Temple. This (understandably) infuriated many Jews, and a family of priests, the Macabees, led a revolt against the Empire. The patriarch of the family, Mattathias, died while resisting the Assyrians, and his son, Judah, took over as leader of the revolt. His followers proclaimed him messiah, and his revolt was partially successful. In 164 BC, he was able to beat back the Assyrians and cleanse the temple, rededicating it to Jehovah. This feat was so important that a Jewish festival was commemorated in its honor. Hanukkah, the Jewish festival of lights, celebrates Judah the Macabee's victory and marks the re-lighting of the Temple's Eternal Flame, which had been extinguished by the Assyrians.[25] Judah the Macabee died later during his revolt, and his named is barely remembered today, even by those who regularly celebrate the festival of Hanukkah.

Jack Gratus, in his book, *The False Messiahs*, summarizes several more would-be messiahs who lived during the time of Jesus Christ. Simon the Slave, Judas of Galilee, the Egyptian Messiah, Theudas the Magician, and many others all claimed messiahship; they all led revolts against the Roman Empire; and they all died for their causes. None of these names are remembered, but Jesus Christ's name is. Why? Some may say that Christ was the most popular of those who claimed messiahship. That is simply not true. The historian Josephus says that the Egyptian Messiah, "...got together thirty thousand men that were deluded by him. These he led round from the wilderness to the Mount of Olives."[26] Christ, even at the height of His popularity, never commanded the attention of anywhere near thirty thousand men!

In fact, one of the most popular of all would-be messiahs was a man called Simon Bar Kochba. He was another insurgent who led an army against Rome in 132 A.D. He called himself the messiah and many agreed with him. The celebrated Talmudist, Rabbi Akiva, called him the "king-messiah." He was so popular among the people and had so much support among the Jewish religious leaders that *coins were minted with his portrait on them!* The portrait showed him holding a pot of manna and the rod of Aaron, obvious symbols of the messiah. Bar Kochba's revolt was quite successful for a time, but he was eventually defeated at the fortress of Bethar. He was then killed for his actions.[27] Christ never had the popular support that either the Egyptian Messiah or Simon Bar Kochba had. Nevertheless, those names and the names of all other would-be messiahs are forgotten, except for Jesus Christ. Why? Because Jesus is unique.

Given the uniqueness of the Bible in its **composition,** its **popularity,** its **survivability**, its **influence**, and its **central character**, any person wishing to learn about the nature of God should at least investigate this important source of information. The Bible's uniqueness does not, of course, prove that it is the word of God. However, it does demonstrate that the Bible is certainly one of the first literary works that should be studied by any person who wishes to consider himself or herself "educated." As Josh McDowell says a professor once remarked to him, "If you are an intelligent person, you will read the one book that has drawn more attention than any other, *if* you are searching for the truth."[28]

ENDNOTES

1. Surah 4:157

2. *The Gideon*, **94:1**, p. 54 (1993).

3. Bernard Ramm, *Protestant Christian Evidences*, Moody Press:Chicago, IL, 1957, p. 227.

4. *The Atlanta Constitution*, July 15, 1993, F 1.

5. *Cambridge History of the Bible*, Stanley Lawrence Grenslade, Ed., Cambridge University Press:New York, NY, 1963, p. 479.

6. *Washington Post*, January 12, 1991, B 7.

7. *Los Angeles Times*, May 27, 1989, II 6.

8. *Washington Post*, Dec. 6, 1989, D 14.

9. Josh McDowell, *Evidence That Demands A Verdict*, Here's Life Publishers:San Bernardino, CA, 1979, p. 21.

10. C. P. S. Clarke, *Short History of the Christian Church*, Longman's, Green, and Company:New York, NY, 1941, p. 10.

11. W. H. C. Frend, *Martyrdom and Persecution in the Early Church*, Baker Book House:Grand Rapids, MI, 1965.

12. *Ibid*, p. 491.

13. *An Encyclopedia of World History*, William L. Langer, Ed., Houghton Mifflin:Boston, MA, 1948, p. 1173.

14. Constantine I had actually ruled the Roman Empire jointly with Galerius in A.D. 305-306.

15. Frend, pp. 518-519.

16. McDowell, p. 20.

17. *Ibid*, p. 20.

18. *The Atlanta Constitution*, August 13, 1991, A 22.

19. T. R. Henn, *The Bible as Literature*, Oxford University Press:New York, NY, 1970, p. 246.

20. Northrup Frey, *Anatomy of Criticism*, Princeton University Press:New York, NY, 1957, p. 316.

21. Cleland B. McAfee, *The Greatest English Classic*, NP:New York, NY, 1912, p. 134.

22. Charles Allen Dinsmore, *The English Bible as Literature*, Houghton Mifflin Company:Boston, MA, 1931, p. 12.

23. Gabriel Sivan, *The Bible and Civilization*, New York Times Book Company:New York, NY, 1973, pp. 144-145.

24. Abraham I. Katsh, *The Biblical Heritage of American Democracy*, (KTAV Publishing House, New York, NY, 1977, *op. cit.*

25. Jack Gratus, *The False Messiahs*, Taplinger Publishing Company:New York, NY, 1975, pp. 20-22.

26. *Ibid*, p. 26.

27. *Ibid*, pp. 53-54.

28. McDowell, p. 24.

Chapter 7
The Historical Validity of the Bible

Now that the rational person has decided to investigate the Bible as a possible source of information concerning the nature of God, how will he evaluate it? How will the rational person decide if this work of literature really does provide insight into the nature of the Creator? Well, the first thing he can do is determine its historical accuracy. The Bible is, after all, mostly a compilation of histories. The works of the Old Testament are mostly histories concerning the Jewish people and the nation of Israel, whereas a good fraction of the New Testament (the Gospels) are histories concerning the person known as Jesus Christ. If the Bible is accurate historically, then perhaps it might also be accurate concerning the nature of God. Alternatively, if the Bible is not even historically accurate, then there's not much hope of it being accurate about something as difficult and esoteric as the mind of the Creator.

It is at this point that the rational person can once again use science as his aid. The archaeological and historical sciences have developed rigorous tests to determine the accuracy of ancient documents which claim to be historical in nature. These tests, called the **Bibliographic, Internal,** and **External** tests, can be applied to any document which contains historical accounts. If the document passes these tests, it can be considered a reliable historical work. All of the history that we currently know concerning ancient times comes from documents which, to one degree or another, pass these three tests.

In this chapter, these three tests are applied to the Bible. If the Bible passes them, the rational person will have strong scientific evidence that its accounts are true. If not, then the rational person should begin looking elsewhere for information concerning the nature of the Creator. Of course, what will be presented in this chapter is only a brief sketch of an historical evaluation of the Bible. An in-depth study requires significantly more discussion than can be provided within the framework of this book. For a more complete historical evaluation of the Bible, the reader is encouraged to examine Josh McDowell's *Evidence That Demands a Verdict*, Volumes I and

II. McDowell does an excellent job of discussing the details of such a study, and this chapter will draw heavily from his work.

The **Bibliographic** Test

When considering the Bible, the first thing that a reader will notice is that most of its historical accounts (excluding the book of Genesis) are written by eyewitnesses. The writers of the books of the Bible recorded the events which took place right in front of their eyes. This is the first requirement of an authoritative historical work.

Eyewitness accounts are, by and large, significantly more reliable than second-hand reports. If, however, we are to believe these eyewitness accounts, we first must make sure that they have not been altered over the course of time. Since we do not have the original documents of any ancient histories, we must find another way of ensuring that the documents we possess today are essentially the same as the originals. The way we do this is to apply the **bibliographic** test.

The bibliographic test simply asks how many different copies of the document exist, and how much time elapsed between the original writing and the first available copy.[1] If several different copies exist and they are all essentially the same, then we can be relatively convinced that each person who did the copying was true to the original text. In addition, the less time that has elapsed between production of the copy and the original, the more reliable the copy is.

Thus, to pass the bibliographic test, a document must have been copied by several different people or agencies, and the copies should have been made soon after the original was written.

In order to see just how well the Bible passes the bibliographic test, we must first see how well other accepted works of ancient history pass the test. For example, the histories written by Cornelius Tacitus are considered very accurate accounts of the events which occurred in the Roman Empire during the first century A.D. His works give us a substantial amount of the facts we know concerning the Roman Empire. Currently, there are 20 copies of his major work (*Annals*) and only 1 copy of a collection of his minor works. The earliest copy of his major work was made almost 1,000 years after the original was written, and the single copy of his minor works was made roughly 900 years after the originals were penned.[2]

By comparison, consider the work of Pliny the Younger who was also an historian of the first century A.D. His *History* is currently supported by 7 different copies, the earliest of which was made 750 years after the original.[3]

For works of ancient history, the numbers quoted above are pretty commonplace. Some works are supported by more copies, some by fewer. The works of Sophocles, for example, have 193 different copies with which they can be compared. This is one of the largest numbers you will ever see in conjunction with ancient works of history. Unfortunately, the earliest of these copies was written nearly 1,400 years after the original.[4] Alternatively, the 850 years which elapsed between the original works of Pliny the Younger and the earliest existing copies represents one of the smallest time spans related to ancient works of history. Compare these numbers to those of the New Testament, which is supported by *over 24,000 different copies*, the earliest of which was written a mere *25 years after the original!*[5] The differences between the 24,000 copies are trivial, indicating that the New Testament we have today is completely faithful to the original text.[6] Let these numbers sink in for a moment. The New Testament passes the bibliographic test *better than any other historical work of its time.*

What about the Old Testament? Does it pass the bibliographic test as well as the New Testament? Not quite, but then again, you wouldn't expect it to. After all, the works in the Old Testament are significantly more ancient. Nevertheless, The Old Testament still passes the bibliographic test better than any other historical document of its time as well.[7] The best way to illustrate this is with the example of the Dead Sea scrolls.

Prior to 1947, the earliest existing copy of parts of the Hebrew Old Testament came from the *Cairo Codex* which was written in about 895 A.D.[8] Since the last events of the Old Testament were supposed to have occurred approximately 450 B.C., this represents a significant time lag between the original writings and the first available copies. In 1947, however, the Dead Sea scrolls were discovered. These scrolls contained copies of parts of at least 500 ancient books.[9] One of the scrolls contained a complete copy of the Old Testament book of Isaiah. The scroll was dated by paleographers as having been written in 125 B.C.[10] This version of

Isaiah "...proved to be word for word identical with our standard Hebrew Bible in more than 95 percent of the text. The 5 percent of variation consisted chiefly of obvious slips of the pen and variations in spelling."[11] In over 1,000 years, then, the book of Isaiah (and presumably the rest of the Old Testament) was copied faithfully. This adds great evidence to the already convincing data which supports the bibliographic reliability of the Old Testament.

In the end, then, the Bible passes the bibliographic test better than any other work of ancient history. As William Green puts it, "...it may be safely said that no other work of antiquity has been so accurately transmitted."[12] Thus, we can be sure that the Bible which we read today is faithful to the original eyewitness accounts. The question remains, however, how accurate are those eyewitness accounts in the first place? After all, the authors of the books in the Bible could have been making it all up. Alternatively, they could have been exaggerating or biasing the events in order to make their religion look better than it really was. That's where the next two tests come in. If the document passes the next two tests, then there is strong scientific evidence that the authors were being truthful.

The **Internal** Test

Now that we are assured that the eyewitness accounts written in the Bible have not been significantly altered over time, we must evaluate this document with the **internal** test. The internal test simply determines whether or not the document contradicts itself[13]. If there are contradictions within the document, then it can hardly be considered trustworthy. However, if no internal contradictions exist, then the document should be further evaluated as a possibly reliable source of historical facts. What about the Bible? Does it pass the internal test? Many people would say that it does not. William Henry Burr, in his book *Self-Contradictions of the Bible*, claims that the Bible contradicts itself at least 144 times[14]. Clearly, if that is the case, then the Bible should not be considered a trustworthy source of history.

Is William Burr right? Is the Bible riddled with contradictions? Well, in the introduction to the 1987 reprint of Burr's book, R. Joseph Hoffman concedes that Burr fails to "...invoke context or linguistic usage"[15] in his analysis of the contradictions. If he would have done so, most of the "contradictions" which he claims to have discovered would have simply vanished.

For example, one "contradiction" he lists concerns the genealogies of Christ[16]. In the New Testament, there are two genealogies of Christ. One is presented in the book of Matthew, chapter 1, and the second is recorded in the book of Luke, chapter 3. At first glance, they seem to be completely contradictory. They don't even agree on Jesus' grandfather. Matthew 1:16 says that "...Jacob begat Joseph, the husband of Mary" whereas Luke 3:23 says that Jesus was the "...son of Joseph which was the son of Heli." One account, then, says that Jesus' grandfather was Jacob whereas another says it was Heli. The fact is, however, that these two genealogies are not contradictory, instead, they are complimentary. The genealogy presented in Matthew is Joseph's family line, whereas the passage in Luke traces Mary's family line[17].

If you understand the culture within which the text was written, this fact becomes clear. Since women were not considered very important to the ancient Jews, their names did not appear in genealogies. Thus, when an historian needed to trace the family line of a woman, he would always use the name of the woman's husband in place of her own name. Most modern translations of the Bible include a footnote to this effect.[18] We see, then, that after examining the cultural context of the passage, this apparent "contradiction" fades away. This is true of many of the supposed contradictions that occur in the Bible.

Other supposed "contradictions" occur because of the difficulty in translating the original languages of the Bible into English. A classic example of this can be found in the New Testament book of Acts.[19] In this book, there are two accounts of Paul's conversion from Judaism to Christianity. Both say that while traveling to Damascus, Paul had a vision of Christ which temporarily blinded him. The accounts supposedly differ, however, concerning the men who traveled with him. In Acts 9:7, the Bible says that "The men who journeyed with him stood speechless, hearing a voice, but seeing no man." However, Acts 22:9 says, "And they that were with me saw indeed the light, and were afraid; but they heard not the voice of Him that spake to me."

Once again, at first glance this seems to be a contradiction. Did the men with Paul hear a voice or didn't they? The answer comes from an examination of the construction of the Greek word (*akouo*)[20] translated as the verb "to hear" in each passage. In Acts 9:7, *akouo* is constructed in the genitive case, whereas in Acts 22:9, the accusative case is used.[21] When this word is used genitively, it implies only that sounds were heard; however, when constructed in the accusative case, the word implies that speech was both heard *and* understood.[22]

In English, we use the same construction for both cases. For example, when a person says, "I hear you, man," he may mean that your voice is reaching his ears, or he may mean that he understands what you are saying. So, once again, a detailed look at these passages yields no contradiction at all. In fact, by looking at both passages we learn something. We learn that Paul's attendants did, indeed, hear sounds coming from Paul's vision, but they could not distinguish any understandable speech from those sounds.

The vast majority of apparent contradictions in the Bible can be simply cleared away by examining linguistic, cultural, and literary context. There are some apparent contradictions that don't have such simple answers, however. An example of this comes from the book of Genesis. In the first two chapters of this book, the creation of the world is discussed. Chapter one gives an overview of the creation, while chapter two goes back and discusses the creation of the world with Adam and Eve as its focus. These two passage seem to differ on the order in which things were created. In Genesis 1:25-27 the Bible says, "And God made the beast of the earth after his kind, and the cattle after their kind...And God said, 'Let us make man'...So God created man in his own image." Thus, according to this passage, the animals of the earth were created first, and then man was created second. In Genesis 2:18, 19, however, we read:

> And the Lord God said it is not good that man should
> be alone; I will make a help-meet for him. And out
> of the ground the Lord God formed every beast of
> the field, and every fowl of the air, and brought them
> unto Adam to see what he would call them.

In this passage, it seems that the animals were created after man, not before him as was stated in the previous passage.

Is this a contradiction? Most likely not. Hebrew is an especially difficult language to translate, because many of the words have several meanings and context is supposed to guide the reader as to how to interpret what is written. It has been suggested by Hebrew scholars[23-24] that a proper translation of the Hebrew verb (*yatsar*)[25] used in Genesis 2:19 is "had formed" rather than simply "formed." If this is the case, then the contradiction disappears. However, the situation is not as clear-cut as was the translation situation in Acts which was discussed above. Although this explanation is accepted by some scholars, it is rejected by others. So, unlike the previous example, there is no conclusive proof that this is not a contradiction. On the other hand, there is also no conclusive proof that this *is* a contradiction.

Do controversial passages such as these keep the Bible from passing the internal test? If they did, then no ancient work of history would pass. It turns out that all ancient works have a few difficult passages that are hard to reconcile with each other. If such a situation is not conclusively proven to be a contradiction, then historians label it a "difficulty." As Robert Horn states, "Difficulties do not constitute objections....Unsolved problems are not of necessity errors."[26] When applying the internal test to ancient documents, historians must follow Aristotle's dictum which says, "The benefit of the doubt is to by given to the document itself, not arrogated by the critic to himself."[27] When these historical principles are applied, the Bible passes the internal test just as well an any other document of ancient history.[28]

The External Test

Once a document passes the internal test, the next test applied is the **external** test. This test determines whether or not the document contradicts any external sources of historical fact.[29] If other histories of the time exist, then the document in question must be consistent with them. In fact, the document in question should, to some extent, overlap with other accepted historical works so as to lend even more credibility to the document. The more overlap that occurs, the better the document passes the external test. In addition to other accepted historical texts, the document in question must also be consistent with any archaeological discoveries for that time period.

Once again, the more archaeological facts that support the document, the better the document passes the external test.

Applying the external test to the Bible is a daunting task because it is a work that covers a long time period. Many parts of the Old Testament report on events that occurred so long ago that they have no external historical works with which they can be compared. In addition, the focus of the Bible is rather narrow; thus, many contemporary historians do not comment on anything related to the Bible's accounts. Finally, a scientist must exert hefty skepticism when examining works that are contemporary with the New Testament, because many of the authors of that time period were sympathetic to the Christian Church. The works of such authors cannot be considered truly objective when they speak of matters reported in the New Testament. In addition, many historical documents written over the New Testament time period were written by Jewish leaders who were vehemently anti-Christian. These accounts must also be taken with a grain of salt.

Reasons such as these lead most historians to consider archaeological discoveries as the primary data used in applying the external test to the Bible. In this chapter, most of the discussion related to the external test will consist of archaeological data, but, nevertheless, we will spend some time comparing the works of external authors to the New Testament. First and foremost, we will reject all works by authors who are sympathetic to the Christian cause. Although many of these authors (Tertullian, Iraneus, Polycarp, etc.) do provide us with accurate portraits of the events of the time[30], their objectivity is in question. After disregarding all of these possibly biased authors, who is left?

Cornelius Tacitus, a Roman, wrote several works which are considered quite accurate histories of the first century A.D. In his major work, *Annals*, he mentions the existence of Christ and his death by Pontius Pilate, in perfect agreement with the accounts written in the Bible.[31] He also mentions certain cities[32] and rulers[33] which are also discussed in the Bible. In each case, Tacitus's reports are consistent with those of the New Testament.

Another well-respected, non Christian historian of the day was Flavius Josephus. Josephus was a Jew who wrote a history of the Jewish people in an attempt to create better feelings between the

Romans and the Jews. In his major work, *Jewish Antiquities*, he not only mentions Christ's death at the order of Pontius Pilate, but he also mentions Christ's resurrection![34] The direct quotation of this reference is presented in the next chapter. Josephus also mentions rulers and cities that are discussed in the Bible, and his reports are also consistent with those of the Bible.[35] In addition, Josephus mentions the life and execution of John the Baptist[36] and the existence of Christ's brother James[37], in agreement with the New Testament.

Two other non-Christian historians who lend support to the New Testament are Thallus and Phlegon. Their contribution to the external test will be discussed in detail in the next chapter. All of these external authors confirm parts of the histories reported in the New Testament. Several more historians who are supportive of Christianity also confirm parts of the New Testament[38], although their support must be viewed with skepticism, as pointed out earlier. The point of this discussion is that the Bible certainly passes the external test with respect to other accepted works of history.

With respect to archaeological discoveries, the Bible truly stands out as an accurate source of history. Whether one is studying New Testament or Old Testament-related data, archaeology provides incredibly convincing evidence for the historical veracity of the Bible. For example, William F. Albright, one of the greatest archaeologists of this century says, "There can be no doubt that archaeology has confirmed the substantial historicity of the Old Testament..."[39] In addition, F. F. Bruce, author and historian, says, "...it may be legitimate to say that archaeology has confirmed the New Testament record."[40]

It would be an impossible task to even briefly sketch all of the archaeological discoveries that have confirmed specific passages in the Bible. As Amihai Mazar, author of *Archaeology of the Land of the Bible*, states, "The digestion of the data uncovered is overwhelming even for professional archaeologists, not to mention scholars of related subjects."[41] Since the volume of such data is overwhelming, we will concentrate on a few specific examples. These examples are ironic, because they represent cases in which archaeologists originally thought that the Bible was in error. More data, however, revealed that the archaeologists were in error, not the

Bible. It is important to note that the following examples are not isolated incidents. As Edwin Yamauchi in his book, *The Stones and the Scriptures*, says, "There are a number of striking cases where specific passages have been doubted...and have [later] been confirmed."[42]

A particularly startling example of such a reversal comes from the Old Testament book of Genesis, chapter 14. This chapter details a series of battles fought between two ancient alliances. During one of the battles, Abram's nephew Lot was captured. Abram led a group of men against the alliance that captured Lot, defeated the alliance, and rescued his nephew. In the early part of this century, most archaeologists believed that this account was a total fabrication. Indeed, in 1918, William F. Albright (quoted above) wrote, "...the Hebrew material was either borrowed from extant legends...or invented by use of haggadic processes."[43]

Since 1918, however, a great number of archaeological discoveries have put the historicity of this tale beyond doubt. Discovery of the Mari Tablets in 1933 provided evidence that the kings mentioned in the account did, in fact, exist and that such long-distance battles were, indeed, fought at that time.[44] In addition, Albright himself discovered significant archaeological evidence that the cities mentioned in the account were at war during that time.[45] In the end, the evidence forced Albright to reverse his earlier belief. In a commentary that he wrote in 1948, Albright wrote, "Genesis 14 can no longer be considered as unhistorical, in view of the many confirmations of details which we owe to recent finds."[46]

The most important aspect of this example is that the same archaeologist who originally doubted the historical accuracy of Genesis 14 ended up being forced to change his mind in light of the evidence. Clearly, Albright did not give Genesis 14 the benefit of the doubt while studying the relevant archaeological discoveries. He believed that it was a fabrication. In the end, however, the data forced him to admit that he was in error. Remember, this is the same archaeologist that was originally quoted as saying that archaeology has confirmed the historicity of the Old Testament. This example provides a lot of credence for such a conclusion. Here is an archaeologist who did not want to believe that the Old Testament was an accurate historical work. However, after a lifetime of archaeological study, he was forced to concede the point. Clearly, he would not make such a statement if the data were not completely convincing.

It is important to note that the Old Testament has been shown by archaeology to be accurate not only in the "big" issues of kings, battles, cities, and dates, but also in "little" issues as well. Archaeologists are constantly being amazed at the Old Testament's accurate attention to detail. For example, in the Old Testament account of Joseph and his coat of many colors (Genesis, chapters 37-47) it is stated that Joseph's brothers sold him into slavery for the price of twenty shekels (Genesis 37:28). Many archaeologists have doubted this price, because, based on early archaeological evidence, slaves sold at slightly later times than Joseph's were significantly more expensive. Once again, however, more archaeological data vindicated the Old Testament. In 1966, the data were so convincing that author K. A. Kitchen wrote,

> ...the price of twenty shekels of silver...is the correct average price for a slave in about the eighteenth century B.C.: Earlier than this, slaves were cheaper (average, ten to fifteen shekels), and later they became steadily dearer. This is one more little detail true to its period in cultural history.[47]

Finally, the New Testament is also just as archaeologically sound as the Old Testament. Consider the case of The Pavement, where the passage in John 19:13 says Christ was tried before Pilate. Prior to about 1950, there was no archaeological confirmation of such a place; thus, many archaeologists believed that it never really existed. In 1960, however, William F. Albright demonstrated that The Pavement was the court of the tower of Antonia, the headquarters of the Roman military. The reason it had not been discovered before was that it had been buried during one of the times that Jerusalem had been rebuilt, and had not been uncovered until the 1950's.[48]

Based on the weight of the somewhat fragmentary historical evidence and the overwhelming amount of archaeological evidence, we can say without question that the Bible passes the external test. In fact, more archaeological attention has been paid to the Bible than any other source of ancient history.[49] Thus, we can therefore say that the Bible passes the external test better than any other source of ancient history!

The unquestionably historical veracity of the Bible

Now that we've put the Bible through the same three tests that are applied to all works of history, we begin to get an appreciation for exactly how historically accurate its accounts are. The Bible passes all three tests, two of them better than any other document of ancient history. The data is too convincing for any unbiased observer to reach a different conclusion. Even many biased investigators see their opinions turned around by the data. Consider, for example, the words of Josh McDowell:

> After trying to shatter the historicity and validity of Scripture, I came to the conclusion that it is historically trustworthy. If one discards the Bible as being unreliable, then he must discard almost all literature of antiquity. One problem I constantly face is the desire on the part of many to apply one standard or test to secular literature and another to the Bible. One needs to apply the same test, whether the literature under investigation is secular or religious.[50]

As the quotation implies, McDowell actually started his historical and linguistic investigations in order to disprove the Bible. Despite this unscientific bias, the data was too overwhelming to refute. The Bible is, quite simply, the most accurate historical work of its time. Although this fact does not tell us that the Bible is "the word of God," what it does tell us is that the accounts contained in the Bible are more historically reliable than any of the other stories we read concerning the same time period. Thus, if you believe in the Roman Emperor Nero and the stories surrounding his rule of the Roman Empire, then you must believe the Gospels of Jesus Christ as presented in the New Testament. The data indicate that the latter belief is more scientifically valid than the former.

ENDNOTES

1. Josh McDowell, *Evidence That Demands a Verdict*, Here's Life Publishers:San Bernardino, CA, 1979, p. 39.

2. *Ibid*, p. 42.

3. *Ibid.*

4. *Ibid.*

5. *Ibid*, p. 43.

6. *Ibid*, pp. 43-52.

7. *Ibid*, pp. 52-60.

8. *Ibid*, p. 56.

9. *Ibid*, p. 57.

10. *Ibid,* p. 58.

11. *Ibid.*

12. *Ibid*, p. 56.

13. *Ibid*, p. 60,61.

14. William Henry Burr, *Self-Contradictions of the Bible*, part of the series, *Classics of Biblical Criticism*, R. Joseph Hoffman, Ed., 1987, p. 90.

15. *Ibid*, p. 10.

16. *Ibid*, p. 56.

17. Josh McDowell and Don Stewart, *Answers to Tough Questions skeptics ask about the Christian faith*, Here's Life Publishers:San Bernardino, CA, 1980, pp. 60, 61.

18. *The Ryrie Study Bible*, Moody Press, Chicago, IL, 1987, p.1549.

19. Burr, p. 67.

20. James Strong, *Strong's Exhaustive Concordance-Compact Edition*, Baker Book House:Grand Rapids, MI, 1983, Greek Dictionary of the New Testament, p. 9.

21. McDowell and Stewart, pp. 16, 17.

22. *Ibid.*

23. E. J. Young, *An Introduction to the Old Testament*, Eerdmans Publishing:Grand Rapids, MI, p. 56.

24. K. A. Kitchen, *Ancient Orient and the Old Testament*, Intervarsity Press:Chicago, IL, 1966, pp. 116-119.

25. Strong, Hebrew and Chaldee Dictionary, p. 51.

26. McDowell, p. 61.

27. *Ibid.*

28. *Ibid*, pp. 60-63.

29. *Ibid*, p. 63.

30. *Ibid*, pp. 63-65.

31. *Ibid*, pp. 81-82.

32. Jack Finegan, *The Archaeology of the New Testament*, Princeton University Press, Princeton, NJ, 1992, p. 129.

33. *Ibid,* p. 139.

34. McDowell, p. 82.

35. Finegan, *opt. cit.*

36. *Ibid*, p. 17.

37. McDowell, p. 83.

38. *Ibid*, pp. 50-52.

39. *Ibid*, p. 65.

40. *Ibid*, p. 66.

41. Amihai Mazar, *Archaeology of the Land of the Bible*, Doubleday:New York, NY, 1990, p. XV.

42. Edwin M. Yamauchi, *The Stones and the Scriptures*, J. B. Lippincott Company:New York, NY, 1972, p.20.

43. Josh McDowell, *Evidence that Demands a Verdict, Volume II*, Here's Life Publishers:San Bernardino, CA, 1992, p. 82.

44. *Ibid*, pp. 83, 84.

45. *Ibid*, pp. 84, 85.

46. *Ibid,* p. 85.

47. *Ibid*, p. 330.

48. McDowell, *Evidence that Demands a Verdict*, p. 73.

49. Mazar, pp. XV, XVI.

50. McDowell, *Evidence that Demands a Verdict*, pp. 73, 74.

Chapter 8
The Question of Miracles

Although the Bible is, from a scientific viewpoint, the most reliable source of history for the time period over which it was written, many still have a hard time believing that its accounts are true. After all, they reason, the Bible is riddled with accounts of miracles, and any rational person knows that miracles simply do not occur! Thus, since the Bible contains accounts of miraculous and supernatural events, its reliability as a source of history must be called into question. Although this is a very popular notion, it simply cannot be supported either scientifically or historically.

Scientifically speaking, we can *never* dismiss any claim simply because it seems miraculous. If scientists did this, then most of the theories of physics which are used today would have never been formulated. Consider, for a moment, the Bohr theory of the atom. This theory leads to the picture of the atom which was presented in Chapter 2. The formulation of this theory led to hundreds of advances in modern physics, yet it is based on an assumption that can only be described as miraculous. In the diagram presented in Chapter 2, electrons whirl around the nucleus of the atom in specific orbits. According to Bohr's theory, those electrons can stay in their assigned orbit, or, with the aid of some outside source of energy, they can move to another orbit. What's miraculous about this theory is that while the electrons are free to travel from one orbit to another, *they are not allowed to pass through any points in between!*[1] Thus, electrons must "blip" out of existence in one orbit and "blip" back into existence in another.

The Bohr theory of the atom is not considered an accurate theory anymore, but it laid the foundations for the modern theories of atomic physics that scientists use today. These modern theories are just as miraculous as the Bohr theory once was. Consider, for example, the following description of how scientists currently describe the inner workings of the proton (one of the particles discussed in Chapter 2) as described in *Science*, arguably the most respected journal in all scientific research:

...physicists already knew the proton's key constituents: three compact objects known as quarks.

Quarks are so much smaller than the proton that they rattle around like a few grains of sand in a vast sea of space. That leaves a lot of room for other kinds of activity...among other things, [these] three familiar quarks are adrift in a surprisingly dense sea of short-lived 'virtual' quarks that *wink in and out of existence.*[2] (emphasis added)

Think about this quotation for a minute. Scientists actually believe that it is possible for things to blip in and out of existence. Can that be described as anything other than miraculous? Nevertheless, this description of the inner workings of the proton is considered today's most accurate theory and continues to guide scientific research. Thus, it is clear that scientists cannot (and do not) reject the miraculous out of hand.

From an historical viewpoint, there are two reasons we cannot discount the miraculous events described by the Bible. First, there are many other historical works which report miraculous events, but their historical validity is never questioned. A quick NABS computer search of 20 major newspapers written from January, 1989 to September, 1993 found several newspaper accounts of miracles. In fact, there were a total of 675 stories that were described by the computer as stories concerning miracles. Of these stories, 33 concerned supernatural occurrences while 29 reported on medical miracles. Many of the remaining stories concerned sporting events and situations in which people were rescued. Three of the medical miracles reported are described below.

The Atlanta Journal Constitution, on October 20, 1990, ran an article on Weston Wells Kilpatrick, a baby that was born with an unrepairable heart ventricle defect.[3] According to the doctors, the baby had no chance for survival. They were terribly upset because there was absolutely nothing that they could do for the child. According to the story, however, the doctors watched in amazement as the heart ventricle defect actually healed itself. Dr. Leonard Bailey of the Loma Linda University Medical center said that it was "...sort of a miracle."[4]

Another major American newspaper, *The Los Angeles Times*, reports on Dawna Munson, who fell into a deep coma after giving birth to twins. Despite the fact that doctors and specialists told the family that death was inevitable, Ms. Munson is alive and well today. Her recovery, as described by her doctor, was "...pretty much a miracle."[5]

Finally, the most amazing of the miraculous events found in the NABS computer search comes from *USA Today*. In its January 30, 1992 edition, there was a story regarding Emma Brady, a woman who was declared dead on January 24, 1992. Doctors decided that she was dead after she failed to exhibit vital signs for 15 minutes. However, one hour later, as her family was saying their last good-byes to her, *Emma Brady began gasping for breath inside the plastic body bag which had been wrapped around her!*[6] She is alive and well today. Doctors have no explanation for this incredible event, and clearly it can only be classified as a miracle.

The point of this discussion is quite simple. If someone were to tell you stories such as these, you would probably not believe them. However, since they are written in newspapers which have strong reputations for accurate reporting, you can be relatively certain that the events described in the stories actually did happen. If you were to find these stories in *The National Enquirer* or *The Weekly World News*, you would be right in questioning their validity. However, if *USA Today* reports something, the story may have a particular bias or slant, but you can be relatively certain that the events which are reported did, in fact, occur. The same exact thing can be said about the Bible. Since the Bible is the *most* reliable source of history for its time period, it eyewitness accounts must be respected.

The second historical reason we cannot discount the miracles reported in the Bible is that some of these miracles have external evidence supporting their historical validity. For example, in Joshua 6:1-20, the Bible reports how the Israelites were able to conquer the city of Jericho. In the account, seven priests led Joshua and his army as they walked around the city on seven different days. The priests blew their trumpets as they walked. On the seventh day, the people of Israel shouted after the trumpets had been blown, and the walls of Jericho fell down of their own accord.

This miraculous event was discounted by most archaeologists until 1936 when Dr. John Garstang discovered an amazing thing while excavating the ruins of Jericho. He was so stunned by what he had discovered that he wrote out a statement and had his two collaborators sign it. A portion of the statement reads as follows:

> ...As to the main fact, then, there remains no doubt: the walls fell outward so completely that the attackers would be able to clamber up and over their ruins into the city.[7]

Think about what this discovery tells us. It tells us that the walls of Jericho were not breached by the acts of an invading army! If that had happened, the walls would have fallen *inwards*. Instead, the walls fell outwards, indicating that either the people inside the city destroyed their own walls (a rather unlikely supposition), or that the walls fell of their own accord, as reported in the Bible.

Another miracle reported in the Bible that is supported by external evidence comes from Matthew 27:45. According to Matthew, the earth was covered in darkness when Christ died on the cross. This miracle has been confirmed from external sources. Julius Africanus, a Christian apologist, quotes an historian named Thallus. Although none of Thallus' works have survived to this time, many other contemporaries do quote him, so his existence as an historian is well-known. According to Thallus, the darkness mentioned in Matthew 27:45 was the result of a full solar eclipse.[8] Another historian of the day, Phlegon, also mentions the same darkness and also reaches for a naturalistic explanation.[9] These two external, non-Christian references indicate that the account in Matthew 27:45 must be right. Obviously, then, we can be assured that this event did, indeed, happen, regardless of its miraculous nature.

Finally, the most important miracle reported in the Bible is the resurrection of Jesus Christ. The historical evidence for this event begins with the account of the resurrection as told by four different eyewitnesses in the Bible. Once again, since the Bible is the most reliable historical document of its time, this means that we must at least consider the possibility that this event did, indeed, happen. We don't have to stop at the Bible, however. We can find a wealth of external evidence to support the historicity of the resurrection account.

Let's first start with the histories of Josephus. As was mentioned in the previous chapter, Josephus was an historian of Jesus' day. Although his histories are not as reliable as those of the Bible, he is nevertheless used as an historical authority of the time and is generally considered a very reliable source of historical information. This is what he has to say concerning Jesus Christ:

> Now there was about this time Jesus, a wise man, if it be lawful to call him a man; for he was a doer of wonderful works, a teacher of such men as receive the truth with pleasure. He drew over to him many Jews, and also many of the Greeks. This man was the Christ. And when Pilate condemned him to the cross, upon his impeachment by the principal man among us, those who had loved him from the first did not forsake him, for he appeared to them alive on the third day, the divine prophets having spoken these and thousands of other wonderful things about him. And even now, the race of Christians, so named from him, has not died out.[10]

Remember, Josephus was not a Christian, nor was he sympathetic to the Christian cause. He was a Jewish historian who was writing to please the Romans[11]. He wrote about the events that took place during his time. According to him, one of those events was the resurrection! Of course, people who do not wish to believe in the resurrection can dismiss both the Bible's and Josephus' accounts, but then they are dismissing two of the most accurate histories of that time. Such a dismissal is not scientifically justifiable.

We needn't stop at two of the most reliable histories of the day, however. There is another incredible piece of external evidence supporting the historical veracity of the resurrection: the empty tomb. As Michael Green aptly puts it, "There can be no doubt that the tomb of Jesus was, in fact, empty on the first Easter day."[12] How can Michael Green be so confident? Well, there is a tremendous amount of external, non-Biblical evidence to support his position. This evidence is so persuasive, that jurists and historians who have examined it end up convinced. For example, an English Barrister by the name of Frank Morrison states:

> In all the fragments and echoes of this far-off controversy which have come down to us we are nowhere told that any responsible person asserted that the body of Jesus was still in the tomb. We are only given reasons why he is not there. Running all through these ancient documents is the persistent assumption that the tomb of Christ was vacant.[13]

This quotation brings out an important point. Most non-Biblical, sometimes even anti-Christian, historical works admit that Christ's tomb was empty. As a matter of fact, they are so worried about its emptiness that they must find a naturalistic explanation for it. This is strong evidence that the tomb was, indeed, empty on the first Easter Sunday.

One external, non-Biblical reference to the empty tomb is called the Nazareth Inscription.[14] It is an edict issued by the Roman Emperor Tiberius between A.D. 14 and A.D. 37 which codifies strict penalties against grave robbers. Most historians agree that this edict was a direct response to Christ's empty tomb and the unsettling effect it had in Jerusalem.

Other examples of anti-Christian references ·to the empty tomb come from Jewish literature. One such first-century document says,

> The disciples of Jesus purloined the body of Jesus before it had been buried twenty-four hours, played at the burial-place the comedy of the empty grave, and delayed the public announcement of the resurrection until the fiftieth day, when the decay of the body had become complete.[15]

A second-century Jewish reference to the resurrection can be found in *Dialogue Against Trypho 108*, which was written in approximately A.D. 190. The reference reads as follows:

> ...one Jesus, a Galilean deceiver, whom we crucified; but his disciples stole him by night from the tomb, where he was laid when unfastened from the cross, and now deceive men by asserting that he has risen from the dead and ascended into heaven.[16]

Both of these references (and early Jewish literature is replete with many more-all the way up to the twelfth century[17]) attempt to explain away the fact that the tomb was empty by saying that the disciples stole the body. Clearly, then, this means that even the opponents of Christianity were willing to admit that Christ's grave was, in fact, empty.

Now, is it possible that the references cited above are correct in their explanation of the empty tomb? Could the disciples have stolen Christ's body and fooled everyone around them into believing that he had risen from the dead? From a scientific point of view, the answer is clearly no. After all, there was at least one Roman guard placed at Christ's tomb, and his sole purpose in being there was to prevent just such a threat. Roman soldiers were well-known for their discipline. For example, Professor George Currie has documented several examples of how Roman guards were treated when found lagging on duty. In one case, a Roman guard who fell asleep while on duty was thrown off of a cliff to his death![18] It is highly unlikely, then, that a band of defeated, unarmed disciples could have overpowered or outsmarted the guard so as to steal Christ's body.

Furthermore, even if this could have happened, is it really conceivable that the farce of the resurrection could have withstood the scrutiny of those in Jerusalem? After all, the entire force of the Jewish leadership was surely occupied in trying to find this purloined body, so as to stop such a devastating attack on their own authority. As John Warwick Montgomery so elegantly states it,

> In AD 56, Paul wrote that over 500 people had seen
> the risen Jesus and that most of them were still alive
> (1Corinthians 15:6). It passes the bounds of credulity
> that the early Christians could have manufactured
> such a tale and then preached it among those who
> might easily refute it by simply producing the body of
> Jesus.[19]

Finally, even if the disciples had managed to steal the body of Christ and then been able to foist a manufactured tale among the people, would they have been able to stand up under persecution if it had all been a lie? Church history tells us that 11 of the 12 disciples (including the one that was chosen to replace Judas) were killed because they preached that they had seen the risen Christ.[20]

Wouldn't at least one of the disciples have admitted to their conspiracy in order to save his own life? Logic, then, dictates that the disciples did, indeed find an empty tomb on Easter Sunday.

There are, of course, other theories as to how the tomb could have been empty without Christ rising from the dead. For example, it is possible that Christ didn't actually die on the cross. Could he not have been in a deep coma when he was put in the grave, and then couldn't he have recovered from the coma while in the tomb? Once again, from a scientific standpoint, the answer is no. Consider the reasoning of Michael Green:

> We are told on eyewitness authority that 'blood and water' came out of the pierced side of Jesus [John 19:26-34]...the eyewitness obviously attached great significance to this. Had Jesus been alive when the spear pierced His side, strong spouts of blood would have emerged with every heart beat. Instead, the observer noticed semi-solid dark red clot seeping out, distinct from the accompanying watery serum. This is evidence of massive clotting of the blood in the main arteries and is exceptionally strong medical proof of death. This is more impressive because the evangelist could not possibly have realized its significance to a pathologist. The 'blood and water' from the spear thrust is proof positive that Jesus was already dead.[21]

So, not only do we have medical proof that Christ did, indeed, die on the cross, it comes from someone who could not possibly have been trying to deceive, because he would have no idea of the significance behind his own words!

Could the apostles and the others who saw Jesus simply have imagined it all? Could they not have wanted to see him so badly that they manufactured an hallucination to give themselves strength and courage to continue their religion? Once again, a scientist would have to say no. Josh McDowell, in his book *Evidence that Demands a Verdict*, does a thorough psychological study on the nature of the resurrection appearances and shows that they do not conform to any known hallucinogenic pathology.[22] Thus, massive hallucinations cannot be used to explain away the resurrection.

In the end, then, the empty tomb is convincing external evidence for the resurrection of Jesus Christ. Its emptiness is an established historical fact, and Christ's resurrection is the only logical explanation for this fact.

In light of all that has been discussed in this chapter, we cannot reject the Bible as an historical document simply because it reports on the occurrences of miracles. It would be both unscientific and ahistorical. Miracles notwithstanding, the Bible is the most historically valid document of its time. In short, if you believe that Julius Caesar was emperor of Rome, you must also believe that Jesus Christ rose from the dead. The latter is a much more scientifically secure fact than the former.

On the subject of miracles, one more important fact should be pointed out. The Creator is, by definition, supernatural. Any book which actually does provide some insight into the nature and character of this Creator should also have some supernatural qualities, should it not? The creation of the universe, communication between Creator and creation, and a description of the Creator must all be, on some level, miraculous. Thus, the miraculous events in the Bible should not dissuade us from our study. Instead, the supernatural character of the Bible should be studied a bit more closely. Chapters 9 and 10 represent just such a closer look.

ENDNOTES

1. Donald A. McQuarrie, *Quantum Chemistry*, University Science Books:Mill Valley, CA, 1983, pp. 34, 35.

2. Faye Flam, *Science* **264**, p. 1843, (1994).

3. *The Atlanta Journal Constitution*, October 20, 1990, A 5:1.

4. *Ibid.*

5. *Los Angeles Times*, December 21, 1991, A 1.

6. *USA Today*, January 30, 1992, A 1.

7. Josh McDowell, *Evidence That Demands a Verdict*, Here's Life Publishers:San Bernardino, CA, 1979, p. 69.

8. *Ibid*, p. 84.

9. *Ibid.*

10. *Ibid*, p. 82.

11. *Ibid.*

12. *Ibid*, p. 218.

13. *Ibid*, pp. 217, 218.

14. *Ibid*, p. 218.

15. *Ibid*, p. 238.

16. *Ibid.*

17. *Ibid.*

18. *Ibid.* p. 213.

19. *Ibid*, p. 224.

20. Hastings, James, *Dictionary of the Apostolic Church*, Vol. II, T and T Clark:Edinburgh, England, 1918, opt. cit.

21. McDowell, p. 199.

22. *Ibid*, pp. 247-255.

Chapter 9
Knowledge From On High

The miracles which are reported in the Bible represent only one aspect of the Book's supernatural character. In fact, many passages in the Bible defy scientific explanation, providing even further evidence of its supernatural authorship. For example, the Bible contains a great deal of information that was not available to the people living during the time in which it was written. It details to the Jewish people many rules and rituals that led to a healthful way of life, long before science studied health issues. How could these things have found their way into the Bible except through the inspiration of some superintellect, like the Creator?

One of the most striking examples of this "knowledge from on high" comes from Genesis 17, verse 10. In this passage, God commands Abraham that all Jewish males are to be circumcised. During the entire period over which the Old and New Testaments were written, Jews were the only people who circumcised their young males. This was one way in which the Jewish people were unique among all of the other tribes of the world. They didn't understand why they were told to do it, they just did it because God said to do it. Medical science today has shown us *why* God told them to do it.

In 1954, a scientific study of 86,214 women living in Boston found that Jewish women were 8.5 time less likely to contract cervical cancer than non-Jewish women.[1] The results of this study were examined carefully, and many medical researchers tried to determine why Jewish women were so much less likely to contract this killer disease. They studied environment, food, and other health-related issues. In the end, two convincing studies showed that Jewish women are protected from cervical cancer due to the fact that they generally have sexual relationships with men who are circumcised![2,3] This is because circumcision makes it much easier to keep the male sexual organ clean. Today, most men in the Western world are circumcised, simply because medical science has shown us that circumcised males are healthier sexual partners than non-circumcised males. Thus, the commandment given to Abraham in Genesis 17:10 was given to him in order to protect Jewish women from a deadly disease.

The Bible not only tells Jews that their males must be circumcised, however, it also says *when* the circumcision must take place. Genesis 17:12 states that the circumcision must occur when the child is eight days old. Once again, ancient Jews had no idea why the Bible was so specific about when a male baby was to be circumcised, but today's medical science tells us that the eighth day of baby's life is the *ideal* time for circumcision.[4] This is because babies tend to have difficulties with extreme bleeding when they are less than 8 days old. The reason for this is twofold.

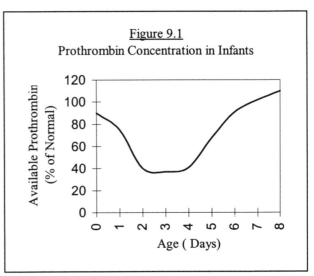

Figure 9.1
Prothrombin Concentration in Infants

First, vitamin K, an important part of the blood-clotting process, is not manufactured in its normal concentration until the fifth to the seventh day of a baby's life[5]. Second, another important chemical for blood-clotting, prothrombin, is available at only 90% of normal concentration when a baby is newborn. Until about day 4 of the baby's life, the prothrombin level actually *decreases* to about 40% of normal, and then it begins to increase in concentration (as shown in Figure 9.1). At the eighth day of life, the prothrombin level is actually 110% of normal. The prothrombin concentration then proceeds to decrease again until it reaches normal levels[6]. Thus, a baby is *more prepared for surgery on its 8th day than at any other time in its life*, because that's when the baby's blood clots most efficiently!

It is impossible that Moses (the generally-accepted author of the book of Genesis) knew about cervical cancer, vitamin K, and prothrombin. Nevertheless, the book he wrote prescribes a surgical procedure that protected millions of Jewish women from a deadly disease. It also prescribes the best time in the life of a male for that procedure to be done. How could he have done that? Could it just be a coincidence? Could Moses have simply dreamed up this procedure and just gotten lucky regarding its results? If this were the only example of such a "coincidence," then that might be the most likely explanation. However, as you look more and more closely at the Bible, you find more and more of these "coincidences."

Consider, for example, the Old Testament's fascination with sanitation. The Bible commands the Jews to relieve themselves outside of their camps or cities by digging outhouses (Deuteronomy 23:12,13). Although this directive sounds like common sense to you and me, it goes against the practices of all other people who lived during those times. Back then, other cultures simply used chamberpots to relieve themselves. When the chamberpots got full, their contents were simply dumped out into the streets. Some people skipped the chamberpot entirely and just relieved themselves in the streets! The revolutionary idea of digging outhouses, as outlined by the Bible, is characterized by medical historian Arturo Castiglione as "...a primitive measure, but an effective one, *which indicates advanced ideas of sanitation.*"[7] (emphasis mine) By following the command of Deuteronomy 23:12-13, the Jews protected themselves from such deadly diseases as cholera, typhoid, and dysentery.

The Bible not only excludes human waste from the Jewish camps and cities, but it also excludes any person who is affected by leprosy. In Leviticus 13:46, the Bible says that a leper must live outside camp limits, and this banishment is to last as long as the individual has the disease. Once again, this directive goes counter to what was done in other cultures but represents a very medically sound rule. The idea of issuing a quarantine to anyone afflicted by a contagious disease has, throughout history, averted many epidemics. As Castiglione puts it, "The laws against leprosy in Leviticus 13 may be regarded as the first model of a sanitary legislation."[8]

Perhaps the most illuminating example of the Bible's advanced ideas of sanitation comes from its commandments to those who come into contact with a diseased or dead body. The Bible says that these people should purify themselves by washing in running water, cleaning their clothes several times, and changing into new clothes that have been washed and dried.[9] With our current medical knowledge, these measures make perfect sense. Anyone who contacts diseased or dead bodies also comes into contact with an enormous number of germs. Those germs can only be eradicated by meticulous washing of both the skin and the clothes. This washing is best done in running water, so that the germs will be whisked away rather than becoming concentrated in a stagnant washing basin.

Even though these measures seem simply common sense to us today, they once again run counter to the ideas of previous centuries. Indeed, until the mid-to-late 1800's, it wasn't even common practice for medical doctors to wash their hands before they treated or examined their patients! This lack of sanitary practice caused innumerable deaths over the centuries. Patients who were unlucky enough to be treated by doctors who had done previous work with diseased or dead people were infected at incredibly high rates.

Things began to change in the mid 1800's, when a doctor named Ignaz Semmelweis became head of the Allegemeine Krakenhaus, a famous teaching hospital in Vienna.[10] During his tenure, it was common practice for teachers and students to begin their day doing autopsies in the morgue and then, without any kind of cleansing whatsoever, they would go to the maternity wards and do pelvic examinations on the women patients. Dr. Semmelweis noticed that the patients who were examined by the teachers and their students were much more likely to become ill and die than the other patients in the hospital. He postulated that something in the dead bodies was being carried over to the women patients by those who had done autopsies. He therefore instituted a rule that forced doctors to wash their hands before examining or treating patients. Many doctors complained that this rule was a real nuisance, but it worked. Maternity ward deaths dramatically decreased.

Surprisingly, Semmelweis' success was not acclaimed by his colleagues. When he left the hospital, his successor rescinded all of the rules regarding handwashing, and the mortality rates in the hospital shot back up. Eventually, Semmelweis wrote a book which documented the fact that patients tended to get sick more often when doctors failed to wash their hands between treatments. As Dr. Semmelweis' work gained recognition and scientific support, physicians began to follow his advice. The same instructions for sanitation which Semmelweis discovered, however, had already been in the Bible for centuries! As medical doctor S. I. McMillen aptly puts it, "At long last...man finally muddled through. He learned, after centuries and at a frightful cost, what God gave to Moses by *inspiration*."[11] (emphasis his)

Again and again, modern medical science has confirmed that following the rules set forth in the Bible will result in a healthful life. The Jewish dietary laws represent another excellent example of this fact. These laws, set down in Deuteronomy 14 and Leviticus 11, outline foods that are not to be consumed as well as methods for preparing food that can be consumed. Based on our medical knowledge today, it is clear that those who followed the Jewish dietary rules would have led healthier lives back in Biblical times. The foods that were forbidden to the Jews, like pork, were impossible to keep free of disease in Biblical times. The methods prescribed in the Old Testament for preparing certain foods, such as keeping dairy products separate from other foods, were clearly the most efficient methods for keeping food as uncontaminated as possible.

Even though we are able to keep foods like those uncontaminated today, medical studies[12,13] show that the Jewish dietary restrictions still result in a positive influence on personal health. The study in reference #12, for example, demonstrates that Jews who follow the dietary laws have substantially less risk for certain types of heart attacks.

How is all of this possible? How could Moses have come up with all of this good medical advice? Certainly not by consulting the medical wisdom of the day. Practicing physicians of Moses' time treated embedded splinters by applying worms' blood and asses' dung. Think of the germs! An Egyptian medical book written near the time of Moses' birth prescribed such wonderful medicines as animal urine, putrid meat, and fly excreta.[14] If Moses didn't get his information there, could he have gotten it through trial and error? Could years and years of trying out new circumcision rituals, new purification schemes, and new eating habits have produced this wisdom? Of course not. As nutritionists have noted over and over again, people of that time had no knowledge of cause and effect between behavior and health[15]. Either Moses was just incredibly lucky, or he was inspired by someone or something that had significantly more knowledge than he or anyone during his time had. In the next chapter, we will see that the inspirer was God.

ENDNOTES

1. W. B. Ober and L. Reiner, *New England Journal of Medicine*, November 30, pp. 555-559 ,(1954).

2. A. Symeonidis, *Bulletin of U. S. Public Health Service* **7**, p. 127, (1959).

3. P.S. Rao, *et al., Journal of the American Medical Association*, November 7, p. 1421, (1959).

4. Martin C. Rosenthal, *Journal of the American Medical Association,* February 13, p. 436, (1947).

5. S. I. McMillen, *None of These Diseases*, Fleming H. Revell Co.: Westwood, NJ, 1963, p. 22.

6. *Ibid.*

7. Arturo Castiglione, *A History of Medicine*, Alfred A, Knopf, Inc.:New York, NY, 1941, p. 70.

8. *Ibid*, p. 71.

9. The rules for ritual cleansing are scattered throughout the Numbers, Leviticus, and Deuteronomy. See for example, Numbers 19.

10. S. I. McMillen, pp. 15-17.

11. *Ibid.*, p. 14.

12. M. Katz, *South African Medical Journal* **50**, pp.2004-2005, (1976).

13. H. A. Kahn *et al., American Journal of Epidemiology* **119**, pp. 775-787, (1984).

14. S. E. Massengill, *A Sketch of Medicine and Pharmacy*, S. E. Massengill Co.: Bristol, TN,1943.

15. Bryna Shatenstein *et al.*, *International Journal of Food Sciences and Nutrition* **44**, pp. 105-121, (1993).

Chapter 10
The Creator's Foresight

Nothing better illustrates the supernatural nature of the Bible than its ability to predict future events. Although the Bible does seem to have a remarkable amount of advanced knowledge (as outlined in the previous chapter), this knowledge did not necessarily have to come from a supernatural source. After all, one could postulate that space aliens visited Moses and gave him the information. Although such an explanation is a bit silly, it has been suggested before![1] Thus, as rational men and women, we must find more evidence that will link the Bible to the Creator.

What better evidence exists than the Bible's uncanny ability to predict the future? The Bible is filled with hundreds of prophecies regarding future events. By now, many of these events have come true, and it is indeed astounding how accurate the Bible is in its predictions. Who could be responsible for these predictions? Certainly no one natural! Everything in the natural world is bound by time. There is no way for anyone or anything that is bound by time to be able to see into the future. Only something supernatural, something unfettered by the constraints of time, would have the ability to accurately predict future events. This characteristic, more than any other, confirms the supernatural aspect of the Bible and links it firmly to the Creator.

You might think that such a statement is too strong. After all, aren't there hundreds of "psychics" that do pretty well at predicting the future? Doesn't the horoscope that you read in the paper have an unnerving ability to describe the events you encounter throughout the day? And what about Nostradamus? Wasn't he a real prophet? How can I use the Bible's ability to predict the future as evidence for its divine origin when all of these other avenues lead to prophetic revelation as well? The answer is simple. The Bible's ability to predict the future is unique among all other "prophetic" sources.

There are two general ways that modern-day prophets attempt to predict the future. One method is what I like to call the "barrage method," and it is generally employed by psychics. When psychics want to predict the future, they generally make hundreds of predictions. They make so many predictions that a few of them are *bound* to come true. When that happens, the psychic's successful predictions are trumpeted while the failed ones are simply forgotten.

For example, Massachusetts psychic Barbara Donchess became famous when she predicted the eruption of Mount St. Helens. Although this success was promoted with great fanfare, her failed prophecies were never discussed. The *National Enquirer* published her predictions for the year 1992 in their January 7, 1992 issue. In the article, Ms. Donchess made 5 predictions which ranged from a member of the royal family testing positive for HIV to Senator Ted Kennedy voluntarily retiring from the Senate and running for Palm Beach Town Council. Not one of the five predictions came true, but she's still hailed as one of America's leading psychics.[2]

In the same issue of *The National Enquirer*, 9 other "leading psychics" gave us their predictions for the year 1992. William Kennedy Smith (the famous Kennedy family member who was accused of rape) was predicted to be so affected by his rape trial that he would become a priest; Americans were supposed to learn that for more than 10 years, the casinos in Las Vegas and Atlantic City have been making a secret gas that keeps people awake so that they can gamble longer; and it was prophesied that one of Clarence Thomas's enemies would release a tape which affirmed Anita Hill's accusations and that, as a result, Justice Thomas would be thrown off the Supreme court. These and 50 other predictions never came true, but the reputations of the psychics remain in tact.[3] Facts such as these illustrate that psychics aren't really prophets, they are simply shrewd con artists.

The other method that modern-day prophets are fond of using is what I call the "fuzzy method." Nostradamus and your daily horoscope are notorious for this. The predictions they make are so vague and general that the reader can interpret them in such a way as to make them come true. How many times has the horoscope said something like, "You will encounter success in your work today." Well, most people encounter some level of success every day at work. Thus, the prediction is bound to come true, simply because it can be interpreted to fit whatever happens.

Nostradamus is considered one of the most successful prophets in the history of the world. He was born in France in 1503 and began making predictions in the early-to-mid 1500's. His prophecies are particularly vague, and this is why he is considered such an excellent prophet. His predictions can be molded to fit nearly any event in history. Consider, for example, this famous Nostradamus prophecy:

> The great man will be struck down in daytime by a thunderbolt. An evil deed, foretold by a bearer of a petition. According to the prediction another is struck at night. Conflict in Reims, London, pestilence in Turkey.[4)]

This prophecy is usually interpreted as a prediction of the assassination of the Kennedy brothers. John F. Kennedy was assassinated with a gun during the day, while his brother was murdered at night. The "evil deed, foretold by a bearer of a petition" supposedly refers to the death threats they both received over the years, and the last sentence of the prophecy is assumed to predict the global unrest which occurred in the wake of the assassinations. As you can see, this kind of prophecy was bound to come true at some point, because it is so vague that eventually, some world event could be fit into it. Prophets such as Nostradamus and astrologers simply use common sense and linguistic manipulation, not a real ability to see into the future.

Contrast these kinds of predictions to those of the Bible. The Bible mentions particular people, particular places, particular events, and particular times. The predictions are detailed and *all of them (so far) have come true!* In the next few pages, I will outline several of the more striking prophecies that the Bible has made. They all come from the Old Testament, because most of the prophecies of the New Testament are not supposed to have come true yet. Some of these prophecies, however, lend direct support to the validity of the New Testament, as will be seen soon.

The prophecies that will be discussed were all written before the events took place. We know this as a result of certain historical facts. First, we know that the entire Old Testament was written by no later than 250 BC, because the Greek Septuigant, a copy of the entire Old Testament, was initiated in the reign of Ptolemy Philadelphius (285-246 BC)[5)]. This is an historical fact. Second, we know from the bibliographic test discussed in chapter 7 that the Old Testament we have today is essentially identical to that text. The date generally-accepted by historians for the close of the Old Testament, is approximately 450 B.C.[6].

The first Biblical prophecy that will be discussed comes from the book of Ezekiel 26:3-21. A subsection of that text says:

> ...therefore, thus says the Lord God, "Behold, I am against you, O Tyre, and I will bring up many nations against you, as the sea brings up its waves. And they will destroy the walls of Tyre and break down her towers; and I will scrape her debris from her and make her a bare rock. She will be a place for the spreading of nets in the midst of the sea, for I have spoken...Also her daughters on the mainland will be slain by the sword...I will bring upon Tyre from the north Nebuchadnezzar king of Babylon...He will slay your daughters on the mainland by the sword; and he will make siege walls against you...Also, they will make a spoil of your riches...and throw your stones and your timbers and your debris into the water...And I will make you a bare rock; you will be a place for the spreading of nets. You will be built no more..."

According to the prophecy, things do not look good for Tyre. As mentioned before, we know for certain that this prophecy had to have been written by 250 BC. The generally accepted date for the writing of this book, however, is 592-570 B.C.[7]. Most historians accept this as a rather strong fact because the book uses a very odd dating system that was only used for a brief time in the early fifth century B.C.[8] Thus, the author was either writing at that time or was a very knowledgeable historian who was doing everything he could to deceive the reader.

Notice how detailed and precise this prophecy is compared to those of modern-day "prophets." Ezekiel calls the city by name. He tells us that many nations will come against her and even singles out the leader of the first nation, Babylon. He is also very specific about Tyre's ultimate fate. He says that Tyre's debris will be thrown into the ocean; it will not be rebuilt; and that it will become a place where fishermen can spread their nets to dry.

94

The other aspect of this prophecy that must be pointed out is the fact that anyone living in Ezekiel's time would consider his predictions to be absolute lunacy. Tyre was one of the greatest cities of the ancient world. According to Dr. Wallace Fleming, Tyre was founded more than 2,000 years before this prophecy was written.[9] During that time, it had grown into the most important trading center in that region of the world.[10]

The city was originally built on a large island which lay one-half mile off the shore of Syria. The island had a nice port where trading ships could dock. A smaller island near the original city was eventually linked to the larger island, making the total circumference of the city approximately 2.5 miles. The outer wall of the city which faced the mainland shore was 150 feet high and was surmounted by battlements. As a result of its prominence as a major trading center, Tyre grew quickly, and an extension of the city had to be built on the mainland.[11] The combination of Tyre's outer walls, its strategic location on an island, and the mainland city as its first line of defense made the city seem invulnerable. In the words of Dr. Fleming, "...Tyre was not only a great city but was considered impregnable."[12]

We see, then, that Ezekiel's prophecy went against the common human wisdom of the day. Had Ezekiel been trying to "make up" a prophecy which would come true, he probably would have tried to predict the fall of a city which seemed a little weaker than the great fortress of Tyre! Instead, Ezekiel pronounced the city's doom, and specifically mentioned many facets of its destruction.

To see just how well this prophecy came true, we only need to consult the history books. According to the ancient historian Herodotus, Nebuchadnezzar, King of Babylon, laid siege to Tyre from 585-572 B.C.[13] In the siege, Nebuchadnezzar was able to destroy and take the mainland city, but he was unable to effectively attack the island city. As a result, he simply laid a 13-year siege, stopping all supplies from entering the island city. This pressure forced Tyre to accept Babylonian rule, but the island city remained in tact. These historical facts are in perfect agreement with the predictions of Ezekiel.

Since Nebuchadnezzar's siege of Tyre occurred very close to when the prophecy is assumed to be written, this particular prediction is not all that impressive. It's possible that the author wrote this "prophecy" after the fact, thereby ensuring its accuracy. Thus, if this were the only prediction made by Ezekiel, it would not be all that impressive. The prophecy continues, however, as does the history of Tyre.

The prophecy states that many nations, not just Babylon, will stand against Tyre. It states that Nebuchadnezzar will destroy the mainland city, but it says that "they" will throw Tyre's stones and timbers into the sea. In using the pronoun "they" instead of "he," the prophecy makes the distinction between Nebuchadnezzar and the others that will stand against Tyre. Thus, the pronoun "they" does not refer to Nebuchadnezzar; it refers to the other leaders which will try to destroy Tyre. As history tells us, other leaders did, indeed, march against Tyre.

In 333 BC, Alexander the Great demanded that Tyre allow him to occupy the island city. The King of Tyre, Azemilcus, was willing to grant Alexander dominion over Tyre, but was unwilling to let him and his army occupy the city. Alexander was thus forced to attack Tyre in order to gain full control over her strategic location.[14] According to the *Encyclopedia Britannica*, Alexander had no fleet with which to attack the island city of Tyre, so he *completely destroyed the mainland city and dumped all of its debris into the ocean.* There was so much debris that Alexander was able to construct a 200-ft wide mole from the mainland city to the island city, making it possible for his army to march straight to Tyre and conquer it.[15]

The mole that Alexander the Great constructed was predicted by Ezekiel almost 250 years before it was built! His prophecy specifically states that Tyre's debris would be thrown into the ocean by someone other than Nebuchadnezzar, and that's exactly what happened! Even the most hardened skeptic would have a hard time arguing that this part of the prophecy was not written down well before the events took place. After all, historians are convinced that the prophecy was written in the fifth century BC. Even if a skeptic is unwilling to believe the generally-accepted date, we know for a fact that the entire Old Testament was copied less than 100 years after Alexander's battle against Tyre. Its very unlikely that a document which was so revered could be altered so significantly and that the altered version could become generally accepted in less than a century! Clearly, this part of the prophecy *had* to have been recorded well before the events took place.

Ezekiel predicted that many nations would march against Tyre, and that's exactly what happened. After Alexander the Great's conquest, the Seleucidae, the Romans, the Moslems, and finally the crusaders all took turns conquering Tyre.[16] After all of this fighting, Tyre lay in ruins. Today, old Tyre is, indeed, scraped down to bare rock. According to historian Nina Jidejian, "The port [of Tyre] has become a haven today for fishing boats *and a place for spreading nets.*"[17] (emphasis mine)

Think about that for minute. Ezekiel's prophecy was so precise that it was able to predict the only future use for the city of Tyre- a place for fishermen to spread their nets out to dry! The prophecy was written down long before Tyre was laid flat by all of its conquerors. Only after about A.D. 600 did Tyre become a haven for the spreading of nets. How can all of this be explained? How could Ezekiel have made such an impressive prediction? Was he just really lucky?

If this were the only example of a specific prophecy in the Old Testament which had come true, then luck might be a reasonable explanation. There are, however, many such prophecies in the Old Testament. For example, Josh McDowell in his book *Evidence that Demands a Verdict*, outlines 11 other Old Testament prophecies which predict the future of other major cities in the ancient world. These prophecies were all written down before the events took place, and they all came true in the smallest detail! How can a rational person explain the Bible's great record in telling the future except by reference to its divine inspiration?

The most impressive predictions that the Bible makes however, concern the life of Jesus Christ. These predictions, called the "messianic prophecies," provide ample evidence for the divine inspiration of the Bible as well as validity of the New Testament itself. The single, unifying theme of the Old Testament is God's promise that He would send a Redeemer to the world. Throughout the Old Testament, there are literally hundreds of predictions made concerning the time that the Messiah would come, the type of person the Messiah would be, the place from which He would come, and His activities on earth. Once again, we can be certain that these predictions were written down at least three hundred years before Christ ever walked the earth, but they are, nevertheless, detailed prophecies which are incredibly accurate.

The most obvious example of the Old Testament's accurate predictions regarding the coming Messiah relates to His birthplace. In Micah 5:2, we read "But as for you, Bethlehem Ephrathah...from you One will go forth for me to be ruler in Israel. His goings forth are from long ago, From the days of eternity." This verse is clearly a prediction that the Messiah will be born in Bethlehem. We know that this verse is talking about the Messiah and not a human ruler, because of the last sentence. No human ruler's "goings forth" are "from the days of eternity."

Interestingly enough, however, there is another Old Testament prophecy, found in Hosea 11:1, which says, "...and out of Egypt I called my Son." Once again, this is clearly a statement regarding the Messiah (no human was ever called God's Son in Old Testament times), but this verse seems to predict that the Messiah would be born in Egypt. This seeming contradiction, however, is easily resolved in Jesus Christ. He was, indeed, born in Bethlehem (Matthew 2:1), but He and His parents had to flee into Egypt to avoid Herod's persecution (Matthew 2:14). He ended up staying there until Herod died (Matthew 2:15). At least 300 years before Christ ever walked the earth, his birthplace and flight into Egypt had already been predicted!

The Old Testament's ability to predict events regarding the Messiah doesn't stop there, however. Another excellent example can be taken from Zechariah 11:12-13. In this passage we read,

> And I said to them, "If it is good in your sight, give me my wages; but if not, never mind!" So they weighed out thirty shekels of silver as my wages. Then the Lord said to me, "Throw it to the potter, that magnificent price at which I was valued by them." So I took the thirty shekels of silver and threw them to the potter in the house of the Lord.

This passage is a lamentation by the prophet Zechariah. He is furious that the people do not value the Lord more highly. In the end, he quotes God as saying that the people think that He (God) is worth only 30 pieces of silver. Those silver pieces are so worthless in God's sight that they should be thrown to the potter in the house of the Lord.

This passage was always a mystery to Jews, until its words were finally fulfilled in the life of Christ. Christ, who claimed to be the same as God (Matthew 27:43, John 8:58), was betrayed by Judas for the "magnificent price" of 30 shekels of silver (Matthew 26:15). Once Judas saw what was happening to Christ as a result of his betrayal, however, he returned to the temple (the house of the Lord) and threw the silver pieces on the Temple floor in a fit of remorse and rage (Matthew 27:5). The priests, knowing that the money was tainted, did not want to put it back into the treasury, so they purchased a field for the burial of strangers. The field was named "The Potter's Field" (Matthew 27:7).

In the end, then, we see that this lamentation of Zechariah was actually a prophecy of some rather intricate details related to Christ's betrayal by Judas. It is truly incredible to think that more than 300 years prior to this betrayal, the Old Testament was able to predict how much it would cost, what would eventually happen to the money, and even the name associated with the final purchase!

Not only are the details surrounding Christ's betrayal accurately predicted in the Old Testament, but specific events regarding His death are as well. For example, Psalm 22:16-18 says, "...they pierced my hands and my feet. I can count all my bones. They look, they stare at me; They divide my garments among them, and for my clothing, they cast lots." These glimpses of Christ's crucifixion, written at least three hundred years before the event, turn out to be incredibly accurate. First, we know that Christ's hands and feet were pierced in order for Him to have hung on the cross. We also know that when a man is hung on a cross, his body is stretched out in such a way as to make his bones (especially his ribcage) much more visible. In addition, John 19:23-24 tells us that the soldiers who had crucified Christ split his outer garment into four parts, and they each took one. When they came to Christ's tunic, however, they found it was seamless, thus, they decided to cast lots to see who would get it. This is yet another example of the Bible's uncanny ability to predict the future.

Another example of the Old Testament's success at prophecy comes from Psalm 34:20 which says, "He keeps all His bones; not one of them is broken." This passage is quite surprising when you think about how the Messiah died. Christ was crucified. When a man is crucified, the way in which he hangs constricts the diaphragm so as to prevent him from breathing. The only way he can take a breath is to push down on the nail that attaches his feet to the cross. By "standing up" in this way, the pressure on his diaphragm is reduced, and the man can gasp for breath. This, of course, compounds the misery of the crucifixion, because the act of pressing down on that nail is intensely painful. Despite the pain, however, the act is instinctive because it is the only way to breathe.

Not only did this fact compound the misery of crucifixion, it also provided an easy way to make sure that the man being crucified was actually dead. When the Roman soldiers in charge wanted to be sure that a man on a cross was really dead, they would break both of his legs. This act prevented the man from being able to push against the nail in his feet, making him unable to breathe. It was therefore common practice for Roman soldiers to break their charges' legs in order to be sure they had died on the cross. The soldier in charge of Christ, however, chose not to break his legs. Instead, he pierced his side with a spear (John 19:33). So, despite the fact that it was highly unusual, Christ was crucified without having any of this bones broken, just as predicted by the Old Testament.

If these were the only Old Testament prophecies concerning the coming Messiah, it would be possible to explain them away as wildly improbable coincidences. According to Josh McDowell, however, there are 332 distinct prophecies in the Old Testament which were fulfilled perfectly in the life of Christ![18] Many of these prophecies are listed at the end of the chapter, along with the details that they predict. Such a large number of prophecies, all written down at least 300 years prior to the life of Christ, provides strong evidence for the supernatural origin of the Bible.

Those who do not wish to acknowledge the divine origin of the Bible might argue that the Old Testament prophecies regarding the Messiah were never actually fulfilled. Instead, the writers of the New Testament books simply concocted all of the details of Christ's life so as to assure that the relevant prophecies came true. This very common argument ignores several key facts.

First, this argument ignores all of the discussion presented in Chapter 7. We have already seen that the New Testament is the most historically valid document of that time period. It passes the historical tests for validity better than any of its contemporaneous works. If you are willing to believe, against the conclusions of historical science, that many of the facts mentioned in the New Testament were just dreamed up, then you are forced to assume that all of the history we know regarding the Roman Empire is also the results of madmen's delusions. This is hardly a scientifically credible position to take!

Second, the argument ignores the fact that most of the writers of the New Testament were rather uneducated. With the exceptions of Paul and Luke, the rest of the New Testament authors had little formal education. Although they probably had some familiarity with the teachings of the Old Testament, they certainly did not have a detailed knowledge of its prophecies. Such things made up the education of Rabbis, not fishermen. Most likely, the New Testament authors didn't even know many of the prophecies that Christ's life fulfilled.

Third, those who argue that the disciples simply altered the facts to fit the prophecies do not realize that many of those Old Testament passages were not recognized as messianic prophecies at that time. As was pointed out regarding Zechariah 11:12-13, ancient Jews did not really understand that this was a prophecy concerning the Messiah. Its meaning was only understood *after* it was fulfilled in Christ. Thus, even if the disciples had wanted to alter the facts to make it look like prophecy was fulfilled, they would not have known which passages in the Old Testament should be fulfilled, so they would not have known what facts to make up!

Finally, if someone wants to believe that the disciples were able to dream up a substantial fraction of the New Testament books and then pass them off as fact, he or she must explain how such a ruse would be possible. After all, the New Testament books were written in the same area that Christ lived and preached. Many of those who read the New Testament books had actually seen, heard, and learned from Christ. How in the world could a bunch of false documents concerning Christ have come to command the respect that the New Testament documents have if they were full of a bunch of lies?

Those who knew better would certainly object. As professor Wilbur Smith pointed out in 1965,

> No one could now issue a biography of Queen Victoria, who died thirty-one years ago, full of anecdotes which were quite untrue. They would be contradicted at once. They would certainly not be generally-accepted and passed on as true.[19]

Since the New Testament documents are quoted as trustworthy and reliable from as early as A.D. 70,[20] it strains the limits of credulity to assume that they are full of stories about Christ that were simply fabrications.

In fact, we know that there are some documents which claim to be biographies of Christ which do contain anecdotes that are simply untrue. The documents, called the "Gnostic Gospels," are full of stories that could not be confirmed by those who knew Christ or knew the disciples. As a result, they were not viewed as accurate by the early church fathers and do not now command the respect that the New Testament documents enjoy.

So we see that the Old Testament prophesied events regarding the life of Christ at least three hundred years before those events took place. In addition, the events prophesied could not have been later fabricated by would-be deceivers. Add these prophecies to the historical predictions discussed at the beginning of the chapter, and the rational person is hard pressed to explain these facts without conceding the divine inspiration of the Bible.

The Messianic Prophecies
(As Compiled by Josh McDowell)[21]

The Promise of a Messiah: Genesis 3:15; Deuteronomy 18:15; Psalm 89:20, Isaiah 9:6; 28:16; 32:1; 35:4; 42:6; 49:1; 55:4; Ezekiel 34:24; Daniel 2:44; Micah 4:1; Zechariah 3:8

The Time He Would Come: Genesis 49:10; Numbers 24:17; Daniel 9:24; Malachi 3:1

His Divinity: Psalm 2:7,11: 45:6,7,11; 72:8; 102:24-27; 89:26,27; 110:1; Isaiah 9:6; 25:9; 40:10; Jeremiah 23:6; Micah 5:2; Malachi 3:1

His Humanity: Genesis 12:3; 18:18; 21:12; 22:18; 26:4; 28:14; 49:10; 2 Samuel 7:14; Psalms 18:4-6,50; 22:22,23; 89:4; 29:36; 132:11; Isaiah 11:1; Jeremiah 23:5; 33:15

His Forerunner: Isaiah 40:3; Malachi 3:1; 4:5

His Birth: Genesis 3:15, Isaiah 7:14; Jeremiah 31:22

His Attention to Non-Jews: Isaiah 11:10; Deuteronomy 32:43; Psalm 18:49; 19:4; 117:1; Isaiah 42:1; 45:23; 49:6; Hosea 1:10; 2:23; Joel 2:32

His Mission: Genesis 12:3; 49:10 Numbers 24:19; Deuteronomy 18:18,19; Psalms 21:1; Isaiah 59:20; Jeremiah 33:16

His Spiritual Graces: Psalms 45:7; Isaiah 11:2; 42:1; 53:9; 61:1,2

He Would be a Priest: Psalms 110:4

He Would be a Prophet: Deuteronomy 18:15

He Would be a Miracle-Worker: Isaiah 35:5,6; 42:7; 53:4

He Would be a Preacher: Psalm 2:7; 78:2; Isaiah 2:3; 61:1; Micah 4:2

He Would be Born in Bethlehem: Numbers 24:17,19; Micah 5:2

Wise Men Would Visit: Psalms 72:10,15; Isaiah 60:3,6

He Would Flee Into Egypt: Hosea 11:1

Herod Would Massacre Children: Jeremiah 31:15

His Ministry Would Center on Galilee: Isaiah 9:1,2

He Would Cleanse the Temple: Psalms 69:9

He Would be Rejected: Psalms 2:1; 22:12; 41:5; 56:5; 69:8; 118:22,23; Isaiah 6:9,10; 8:14; 29:13; 53:1; 65:2

He Would be Persecuted: Psalms 22:6; 35:7,12; 56:5; 71:10; 109:2; Isaiah 49:7; 53:3

He Would Enter Jerusalem on a Donkey: Psalms 8:2; 118:25,26; Zechariah 9:9; Daniel 9:24-27

He Would be Betrayed by a Friend: Psalms 41:9; 55:13; Zechariah 13:6

He Would be Betrayed for 30 Silver Pieces: Zechariah 11:12

His Betrayer Would Die: Psalms 55:15,23; 109:17

The Betrayal Price Would Buy the Potters Field: Zechariah 11:13

He Would be Deserted by His Followers: Zechariah 13:7

He Would be Falsely Accused: Psalms 2:1,2; 27:12; 35:11; 109:2

He Would be Silent Before His Accusers: Psalms 38:13; Isaiah 53:7

He Would be Mocked: Psalms 22:7,8,16; 109:25

He Would be Beaten, Spit On, and Scourged: Psalms 35:15,21; Isaiah 50:6

He Would be Patient Under His Suffering: Isaiah 53:7-9

He Would be Crucified: Psalms 22:14,17

He Would be Given Gall and Vinegar on the Cross: Psalms 69:21

He Would Pray for His Enemies: Psalms 109:4

He Would Die in the Prime of His Life: Psalms 89:45; 102:24

He Would Die with Malefactors: Isaiah 53:9,12

Nature Would React to His Death: Amos 5:20; Zechariah 14:4,6

Soldiers Would Gamble for His Clothing: Psalms 22:18

His Bones Would not be Broken: Psalms 34:20

He Would be Pierced: Psalms 22:16, Zechariah 12:10; 13:6

He Would Die Voluntarily: Psalms 40:6-8

He Would Suffer Vicariously: Isaiah 53:4-6,12; Daniel 9:26

He Would be Buried with the Rich: Isaiah 53:9

He Would Rise from the Dead: Psalms 16:8-10; 30:3; 41:10; 118:17; Hosea 6:2

He Would Ascend into Heaven: Psalms 16:11; 24:7; 68:18; 110:1; 118:19

ENDNOTES

1. Erich von Daniken, *Chariot of the Gods*, Bantam:New York, 1971, pp. 34-41.

2. *The National Enquirer*, January 7, 1992, p. 24.

3. *Ibid,* pp. 24-25.

4. Erika Cheetham, *The Final Prophecies of Nostradamus*, Putnam Publishing:New York, NY, 1989, p. 54.

5. Josh McDowell, *Evidence That Demands a Verdict*, Here's Life Publishers:San Bernardino, CA, 1979, p. 144.

6. *Ibid.*

7. Joseph Free, *Archaeology and Bible History*, Scripture Press Publications:Wheaton, IL, 1950.

8. *Ibid*, p. 226.

9. Wallace B. Fleming, *The History of Tyre*, Columbia University Press: New York, NY, 1915, p.8.

10. *Ibid*, p. 14.

11. *Ibid*, p. 4.

12. *Ibid*, p. 8.

13. *Ibid*, p. 44.

14. *Ibid*, p. 54.

15. *Encyclopedia Britannica*, 1970, Vol 22, p. 452.

16. Fleming, pp. 65-122.

17. Nina Jidejian, *Tyre Through the Ages*, El-Mashreq Publishers: Beruit, 1969, p. 139.

18. McDowell, p. 175.

19. *Ibid*, pp. 189-190.

20. *Ibid,* p. 51.

21. *Ibid*, pp. 175-176.

Chapter 11
Some Final Thoughts

In the preceding chapters, I have outlined the scientific case for Christianity. I have shown that everything we know in natural science points to the existence of a Creator. I have demonstrated that historical science supports the Bible as the best source of information regarding this Creator. Finally, I have discussed how the information contained in the Bible itself provides significant evidence for its divine inspiration. In short, I find the scientific case for Christianity is very, very strong.

If it really is that strong, however, why don't more scientists believe in Christianity? Scientists are supposed to be unbiased observers who look only at the facts and then draw what conclusions they can from those facts. If the facts point so clearly to the validity of the Christian faith, why aren't more scientists persuaded? This is a very good question. It is a question that I confess I have spent a great deal of time puzzling over. In the end, I think the best way to answer this question is to discuss my own personal experiences as one who was first a scientist and then a Christian.

From the time I was in second grade, my teachers noticed that I had an aptitude for mathematics and science. As a result, they pointed me in that direction. I was given extra research projects to do, extra math concepts to learn, and many, many extra books to read. All of these extra lessons allowed me to learn many things. One lesson that seemed to repeat over and over again was that scientists do not believe in God. As I look back, I'm not exactly sure how this message was imparted to me, but it was, nevertheless strongly imparted. Perhaps part of it was the fact that none of my schoolwork ever had anything to do with religion - any kind of religion. Perhaps part of it was the fact that while my atheistic teachers were allowed to share their beliefs with me and were able to encourage me to believe likewise, my Christian teachers were not allowed to do so, because of the ever-present "separation of church and state." As a result, the only religion I learned from my early scientific role models was atheism.

My parents, of course, were strong Christians and tried to encourage me to believe likewise. They forced me to go to church, but I had been so brainwashed by my early education that I simply shut my mind to any religion other than atheism. In the end, I figured that Christianity was good enough for those who didn't know any better, but for a scientist such as myself, religious nonsense was simply inexcusable.

When I finally reached high school, I was a full-fledged atheist. I was so proud and confident of my position that I actually led an atheist discussion group that met one day a week after school. We read all of the great atheistic philosophers, from Russell to Nieztche and spent the rest of our time bashing religious people. One day, however, a friend of mine asked me to accompany her to a debate that was being sponsored by a Christian group called Campus Life. The debate was on the existence of God. I was very reluctant to go at first, but in the end, I decided that I might learn a few arguments from the atheist debater, so I decided to go.

My first surprise was to find that both debaters were scientists. The atheist was a professor of biology while the Christian was a professor of physics, and both of them taught at very prestigious universities. I was, quite simply, in shock that a professor of physics could actually believe in Christianity. My education had made it clear up to that point that real scientists were all atheists! What was this professor of physics doing up there defending something as unscientific as Christianity?

I honestly don't remember many of the details concerning the debate. I can't even tell you who, in my mind, won. I only remember one exchange between the two sides. The atheist said that it was the scientist's job to try and reach a naturalistic explanation for the world around him. Everything that we can see, hear, or touch had to be explained in terms of natural causes. Any reference to a supernatural being, in the end, was simply a cop-out - an admission of ignorance. The Christian, on the other hand, said that a scientist's job was to look at all of the facts in an unbiased way and draw the most logical conclusion based on those facts. He then looked out into the audience and said that he challenged anyone out there who claimed to be a rational person to investigate all of the facts. He was confident that anyone who looked at all of the facts would, in the end, believe in Christianity.

I never spoke to either of the debaters. I can't even remember their names. But I did take the professor of physics' challenge. All of my life, up to that point, I had only looked at the facts on one side of the issue, the atheist's side. In response to his challenge, I began to look at the facts on the other side of the issue as well. I read the works of Christians such as Josh McDowell, Peter Stoner, and F. F. Bruce. I also studied other world religions like Islam, Buddhism, and Hinduism. At the same time, I read the works of atheists like Steven Gould, Carl Sagan, and Peter Atkins. In short, I gathered up as many facts as possible on both sides of the issue. In the end, the data, much of which has been presented in the previous chapters, were very clear. Although I had been taught all of my life that the only scientifically sound belief was atheism, I found that science itself pointed unmistakably towards the existence of God. Furthermore, the God that science points to is clearly the God of the Old and New Testaments.

These realizations, however, were not enough to bring me to faith in Christ. Although the scientist in me was convinced, it took a significant emotional issue in my life to make me admit that I had been wrong all of those years and to force me to finally take the "leap of faith" that I mentioned in the introduction to this book. Although I do not wish to write about the emotional issue that lead me to make this final leap, I am convinced that the leap would have not been possible if the scientist within me had not been first persuaded by the preponderance of the data. Thus, I owe my faith in Christ, as well as my scientific integrity, to a professor of physics whose name I cannot even remember.

Based on my own experience, then, I can come up with several reasons why more scientists are not Christians. The first reason is that we are simply indoctrinated at a very early age to become atheists. As I said before, my Christian teachers could not express their faith to me or point me towards any scientific reading material that validated their faith because public schools are supposed to be "free of religion." The problem with such an absurd notion is that something must fill the void that is left behind. Since atheism is a belief system that can be discussed in school, and since teachers can assign readings by atheistic scientists, atheism becomes the religion of the public schools. This situation, almost certainly unintentional on the part of the public schools, is necessarily the result of trying to take religion out of school.

This ridiculous situation continues in college. At the University of Rochester, where I attended both undergraduate and graduate school, I spent hours in physics, chemistry, and mathematics lectures where the professor openly ridiculed religion. Despite the fact that many of my other science professors were religious, they were not allowed to provide balance to this barrage of dogma. As a result, the overwhelming conclusion any budding scientist will come to after attending such a university environment is that scientists do not believe in God.

The next reason is a consequence of the first. Those of us who do retain religious conviction are regularly ridiculed on the college campuses. This became very apparent to me when I entered graduate school. At that time, I had to choose a professor who would be my research advisor. His role was to direct my research and provide me with the training necessary to become a scientist in my chosen field. I picked my research advisor based on the kind of work that he did. The man I chose did what I considered to be the most interesting chemical research that went on at the University of Rochester.

While he was, in fact, an incredibly gifted scientist, my chosen research advisor was an atheist. As my Christian views became apparent to him, he ridiculed them. In addition, one of the other members of our research team, a man I still consider to be the greatest scientist I have ever worked with, also constantly made fun of my religious beliefs. Such a situation was very difficult for me. After all, I admired these two men. I aspired to become the caliber of scientist that they both were. Nevertheless, they made fun about the most important thing in my life! Throughout my graduate school career, I concluded that if I was not as strongly convinced as I was by the data, I would have left my religious convictions behind to escape the ridicule of these scientific role models.

The third reason stems from the fact that most of the scientists I know have never investigated the data. There is, of course, a very good reason for this. Any time that a scientist spends researching something that is not directly related to his field, the less likely that person is to become a great scientist. Today's science is so

110

intricate and so specialized, that a person must devote himself completely to his field, or he will be left behind. Thus, since scientists have been indoctrinated over the years to believe that atheism is the only scientifically sound belief system, they are not about to waste time and energy researching the facts surrounding the issue. The wasted time would damage their careers too severely.

Quite simply, as a result of writing this book, I am not as well-known or well-respected a scientist as I could be. The time spent in compiling and writing this book has taken away from time I could have spent in other scientific research. All scientists face this difficulty in trying to devote some time to an interest outside of their chosen field. This reason, more than any other, hinders practicing scientists from becoming Christians.

In addition to the time constraints that inhibit scientists to examine questions outside of their field, there is a definite pressure in the University setting to either not believe in religion at all or, if you do believe, to keep quiet about it. For example, a professor of biology at San Francisco State University was forbidden to teach the introductory biology that he had been teaching for more than a decade because he began stressing the design elements that are prevalent in the world around us. The biology department felt that this would "confuse" students when they later reached a course on evolution, so they forbade him to teach that course![1]

As a Christian professor, I personally felt great pressure from my own department to keep quiet about my religious views. Several of my colleagues openly ridiculed me for my beliefs. I was an outcast in my own department. After a while, I decided that there was really very little academic freedom in today's universities, and I left to pursue a career in the private sector. Despite the fact that I had the best teaching evaluations and one of the most prolific research programs in the department, I left because it became clear that there was no chance for me to reach tenure due to the discrimination prevalent in today's universities.

In the end, then, scientists are indoctrinated at a very early age to be atheists; they are ridiculed throughout their careers if they believe otherwise; they usually cannot spare the time necessary to look into the facts regarding other belief systems; and they are often punished for believing anything but the accepted university dogma.

These issues keep scientists from learning the data necessary to help them understand the relationship between science and Christianity. As a result, only a few scientists are Christians. The rest of the world sees this and is forced to conclude that Christianity must be unscientific. I hope this book has been able to combat this unfortunate situation in some small way.

If you have gotten this far in reading this book, I can only conclude that you have chosen to spend the time necessary to look at the facts. I applaud you. I caution you, however, that your journey is only partially complete. If you truly want to make an intelligent, scientific decision, you must do more research. Read a book written by an atheistic scientist such a Steven Gould. Then read a book written by a scientist who is a Christian. *What is Creation Science* by Henry Morris and Gary Parker would be a good place to start. To investigate historical data further, start with Josh McDowell's *Evidence That Demands a Verdict*. In short, gather all of the facts that you can from both sides of the issue. If you do this, I am confident that the data will speak for itself, and you will end up believing in Christianity. **Godspeed on your journey!**

ENDNOTE

1. Constance Holden, *Science* **262**, pp. 1976-77 (1993).

INDEX

About the Author

Dr. Jay L. Wile lives in Anderson, Indiana with his loving wife, his wonderful daughter, and his two moody cats. He holds an earned Ph.D. in nuclear chemistry from the University of Rochester. His teaching credits include the University of Rochester, Indiana University, the Indiana Academy for Science, Mathematics, and Humanities, and Ball State University. Dr. Wile has published more than 30 scientific articles in the peer-reviewed journals of his field and has lectured extensively on Christian Apologetics and the Creation/Evolution Debate. He is currently the Senior Programmer/ Analyst at Indiana's premiere medical laboratory, Pathologists Associated. In his "spare time," Dr. Wile develops high school science curricula for homeschoolers.

Dr. Wile is willing to speak to any organization interested in hearing the results of his research on Christian Apologetics, the Creation/Evolution debate, or the importance of home schooling. If you would like Dr. Wile to speak at your organization, please contact him at:

Apologia Educational Ministries
808 Country Club Lane
Anderson, IN 46011
jlwile@highschoolscience.com
www.highschoolscience.com